CHILD ABUSE & NEGLECT:
A GUIDEBOOK FOR EDUCATORS & COMMUNITY LEADERS

2ND EDITION

Edsel L. Erickson
Western Michigan University

Alan W. McEvoy
Wittenberg University

Nicholas D. Colucci, Jr.
University of Southern Maine

LEARNING PUBLICATIONS, INC.
Holmes Beach, Florida 33509

Library of Congress Catalog Card Number:
78-059726

Hardcover: ISBN 0-918452-75-9
Softcover: ISBN 0-918452-62-7

Learning Publications, Inc.
PO Box 1326
Holmes Beach, Florida 33509

Cover Design by Rob Gutek

Printing: 2 3 4 5 6 7 8 Year: 5 6 7 8

Printed in the United States of America

62.7
n 4

Acknowledgments

We would like to express our gratitude to all those professionals and lay persons who have contributed to the development of knowledge in the area of child abuse and neglect. The considerable work done by child protective agency persons, educators, social workers, counselors, physicians, law enforcement agencies and private organizations has greatly assisted us in writing this book. Their sensitivity and humanism represent a powerful force in helping to overcome a serious problem.

We would also like to thank Barbara McFadden, Nedra Zerbel, Sue Dickerman, Susan Wiltse, Betty Thompson, Leila Bradfield, Danna Downing and Lois Carl for their expert advice and editorial assistance. Their insight and unceasing good cheer are much appreciated.

Finally, we would like to give special thanks to Ruth Erickson, Janice McEvoy and Ara Colucci whose love and support are paramount in all our endeavors.

Table of Contents

Part A
The Need For
School Involvement

1

Involving Schools

[Child abuse and neglect is a problem affecting not only families but entire communities. Although child maltreatment is not new, the seriousness of the problem has begun to arouse considerable attention at the local, state and national level. Since the early 1970s, all fifty states have passed laws concerning the reporting of child abuse and neglect with special provisions for assisting children and their families. Yet it is at the local level, depending upon the actions of a variety of groups in the community, that intervention efforts will meet with success or failure. The success of any community program to remedy child maltreatment is contingent upon the willingness of school personnel, medical and legal professionals, and human service workers to cooperate with one another.]

Any comprehensive approach to the treatment of child abuse and neglect must heavily involve the schools. There are two compelling reasons for school intervention. First, it is very inexpensive, wtih no change needed in academic goals or resource allocation. Second, because abuse is developmentally damaging to children, intervention is an educationally sound practice. Given that educators often represent the "front line troops" who have regular contact with children outside the home, considerable demand has been placed upon them to be involved in the identification, therapy and prevention of child maltreatment. Despite the importance of involving educators, many schools have not been as effective as they could be in alleviating the problem. Though the reasons for this past oversight are understandable, the problem will only persist with inattention.

REASONS FOR SCHOOL NEGLECT

To a certain extent, administrators, teachers and school staff have, until recently, been unaware of the magnitude of abuse and neglect that exists in our society. This is understandable. Evidence suggests that it wasn't until the 1960s that child abuse and neglect was "discovered" as a significant and widespread social problem. Prior to that time, so little attention was given to the problem that even physicians encountering severely battered children failed to recognize the etiological factors involved and the condition was labeled "unspecific trauma" (Pfohl, 1977).

In addition to the lack of information concerning the problem, past tendencies of school personnel not to report suspected cases of abuse and neglect can be understood in the context of cultural assumptions surrounding parent-child relationships. Conventional wisdom suggests that it is "natural" for parents to love their children and protect them from harm. It is inconceivable for most people to accept the idea that large numbers of parents will purposely hurt their children. Maltreatment of children violates the stereotype of benevolent parenthood.

Similarly, it is part of our culture that parents can and should physically punish their offspring. The old statement "Spare the rod and spoil the child" reflects a tradition which legitimatizes physical punishment of chldren by parents. Many also expect teachers to physically punish children when they exhibit certain misbehaviors. Moreover, the recent Supreme Court decision supporting the use of corporal punishment in school gives further testimony to its legitimacy. Even so, there is considerable disagreement among educators and others over what constitutes proper punishment at school or home. What is considered "good" discipline from one perspective might be construed as "abuse" from another. As a consequence, a precise and generally acceptable definition of abuse beyond that of "battering" children is difficult to provide. Some experts contend that these different standards for child rearing and the ambiguities associated with physical punishment have contributed to the problem of abuse and neglect.

In conjunction with this, there is the commonly held value that educators should not interfere with the authority of parents to discpline their children in ways they prefer. As such, there are educators who are understandably reluctant to involve themselves in child rearing practices for fear of raising the ire of parents and being accused of usurping parental authority. Schools, in the past, could also rightly fear that should they report a suspected case of abuse or neglect, the parents might instigate legal action against them. Schools, like other organizations, are loath to become involved in the litigation process. Today, however, schools are protected from such legal entanglements.

Nevertheless, past fears may still persist and act as a deterent to educators who might otherwise want to intervene in the family life of their students.

Another dimension of the "noninterference with parents" ethic has to do with limited conceptions of the rights and obligations of teachers and school administrators. There are many who believe that a school's responsibility to a child has been and continues to be limited to teaching basic skills such as reading and mathematics and clearly does not extend beyond the confines of the classroom. Dealing with family problems or "patient diagnosis" is perceived by some as outside the realm of the school staff's professional academic duties. Ironically, many feel it is quite appropriate for school staff to report suspected cases of hyperkinesis, dyslexia, retardation, etc. which may contribute to learning problems, yet abdicate responsibility when it comes to child abuse and neglect which also affect learning. This rather truncated definition of school staff roles still contributes to the lack of school involvement in the reporting process.

Another reason for limited involvement in abuse and neglect may be the fear that a school's reputation or an educator's prestige can be tarnished if word gets out that the school is affiliated with such "deviant" parents. Even in instances where some school personnel wish to report suspected cases, they may encounter problems with other staff who wish to protect the school's image. This "head in the sand" approach can be extremely detrimental to ameliorative efforts. It is our contention that a school's reputation is actually enhanced if school personnel are actively involved in community efforts to deal with the problem. Furthermore, school systems have a legal mandate to protect teachers or other school staff who report suspected child abuse and neglect cases, even when their immediate superiors instruct them not to do so.

Perhaps the single most important reason why schools have not been as helpful as they could in the past is the fact that teachers, administrators and supportive staff have been uninformed about procedures for identifying, reporting, and following up on abuse and neglect cases. In-service training (instruction) concerning the laws surrounding child abuse and neglect, indentification of symptoms of different types of abuse and neglect, specific procedures for reporting cases, as well as information concerning community agencies dealing with abuse and neglect, etc. are inadequate or altogether absent in many school systems. Moreover, even those who are still being prepared for teaching are not receiving adequate preparation as reflected in a recent study by the Education Commission of the States (1977). It was reported that the teacher education programs investigated spent an average of less than three hours instruction in the area of child abuse and neglect. Given the complexity of the problem and such superficial instruction, it is no wonder that schools have been rather passive about child abuse and neglect.

Despite all the reasons for school non-involvement, it is our belief that school systems are becoming increasingly involved in efforts at primary and secondary prevention of child abuse and neglect in the community (Garbarino and Gillian, 1980). Educators are realizing more and more that child abuse and neglect is a problem within every community and that they have both the right and the obligation to become involved. Teachers, administrators, school nurses, psychologists and counselors realize that the whole family unit is part of their professional domain, especially if the child is in physical danger or suffering emotional or learning problems as a result of the family situation. In light of the fact that a large percentage of the abused and neglected children are of school age, the potential contribution of the school in eliminating the problem is enormous. The child's right to protection is one of the primary concerns of every socially conscious school. However, concern is not enough to solve the problem. Intelligent planning and action, based upon collaboration with the community, is required for the schools to achieve their potential in helping children.

THE NEEDS OF EDUCATORS

Unfortunately, schools are nowhere near realizing their potential for lessening either the occurrence or effects of child abuse and neglect. This is due in part to a lack of coordinated planning with other community agencies. Educators need to be very clear about how they can offer their services to the community while still accomplishing their traditional goals. In our schools, educators are struggling to balance their social and academic responsibilities so that they can respond to the unique needs of their clientele. In this regard, unless educators deal more effectively with child abuse and neglect, they will be unable to fully carry out either their social or academic responsibilities.

There is no doubt that educators are becoming increasingly conscious of the problem of child maltreatment which this nation is beginning to address. Furthermore, they are being sensitized to identify and report on the signs of maltreatment. In fact, in some parts of the country, referrals to child protective agencies from schools are taxing resources to the breaking point. Due to the limited resources of child protective services in many communities, schools are often placed in the precarious position of having to wait days or weeks for agencies to act upon a suspected case once a report is filed. Even more troubling than the limited services available is the fact that the majority of abuse and neglect cases are never reported.

Two obvious conclusions might be added to these statistics. The first is that more resources should be allocated
to child protection agencies. The second is that further
work needs to be done to foster more effective identification and reporting than has been the case to date. However,
even if sufficient funds and trained staff can be found for
child protection agencies—and that is doubtful—and even
if every case of abuse and neglect was reported, there would
still be important work for educators.

For example, school staff need to be willing and trained
to effectively assist child protection agency professionals
and other groups in protecting children and preventing
abuse and neglect. This is a very practical and important
matter for educators. The way they relate to others in the
community concerning maltreatment will have consequences for all of their students.

AN OVERVIEW

This book goes beyond a mere description of the history
and magnitude of child abuse and neglect in this country,
definitions of abuse and neglect, characteristics and needs
of abusers, requirements for district-wide and school building policies, and the need for reporting. While dealing with

these issues, this book also addresses the question of "what then" after reporting has occurred. Hopefully, this book will encourage the development of knowledge and skills which enhance the effectiveness of educators when they encounter formerly and currently abused and neglected children and their parents.

Much of the attention of schools, the public media, professional communications and in-service programs is still being limited to a sensitization of the problem—particularly of battered children. While there is a continuing need to advance public awareness and encourage reporting, there is also a great need for suggestions that describe how schools can help prevent abuse from occurring in the first place. This book offers a number of specific strategies for schools to employ in the area of prevention.

As a prelude to the "what then" of therapy and prevention programs, we summarize the literature and laws in chapters 2 and 3 on the magnitude of child abuse and neglect, and what parents who abuse or neglect their children might be experiencing. However, incest represents a special case of child abuse in terms of its dynamics and consequences. We therefore treat incest separately in *Chapter 4.*

In *Chapter 5,* we focus on recommendations for the development of school policies, i.e., policies for identifying and reporting abuse and/or neglect, policies for the coordination of community and school personnel, and policies for the development of professional activities. We are particularly interested in fostering policies that are likely to be implemented, and in this vein, offer suggestions which may facilitate community-wide support for putting into effect desired programs. In *Chapter 6,* we offer a detailed discussion of how maltreated children can be identified. In *Chapter 7,* we discuss how to report such children to child protective service agencies.

In *Chapter 8,* our discussion deals with the roles of school building administrators, nurses, social workers, psychologists, counselors and teachers after child abuse has been identified and reported. Particular consideration is given to the manner in which school staff should and should not relate to the parents of maltreated children and to the children themselves. In *Chapter 9,* special attention is given to the potential roles of school health workers, i.e., school counselors, psychologists, social workers and nurses, in providing preventive services so that the community—through protective services—does not have to intervene to safeguard the welfare of children.

In the last part of the book, school curriculum programming for preventing child abuse and neglect is examined. Consideration is given in *Chapter 10* to a variety of activities which can be conducted within a community.

education framework or within regular elementary and secondary programs.

The last chapter *(Chapter 11)* is specifically addressed to one very important contribution schools can make through a program for teenage parents. It examines how existing programs or the lack of programs may inadvertently contribute to child abuse and neglect. Suggestions are offered which some educators believe will lessen the likelihood of abuse and/or neglect among teenage parents.

We believe that with careful planning and proper use of resources, schools can respond effectively to the challenge of child abuse and neglect. This book provides a framework for addressing that challenge.

SUGGESTED READINGS

Finkelhor, David, SEXUALLY VICTIMIZED CHIL-
DREN. New York: Free Press, 1979.

Garbarino, James and Gillian, Gwen, UNDERSTAND-
ING ABUSIVE FAMILIES. Lexington, MA: Lexington
Books, 1980.

Helfer, R. E. and Kempe, C. H. (Editors), CHILD ABUSE
AND NEGLECT: THE FAMILY AND THE COM-
MUNITY. Cambridge, Massachusetts: Ballinger Pub-
lishing Co., 1976.

Hill, D., COMMUNICATION AND COLLABORATION
IN DEVELOPING APPROACHES TO CHILD
ABUSE PREVENTION AND TREATMENT. In Fifth
National Symposium on Child Abuse. Denver, Colo-
rado: American Human Association, 1976.

Kline, Donald F., CHILD ABUSE AND NEGLECT: A
PRIMER FOR SCHOOL PERSONNEL. Reston, Virginia: The Council For Exceptional Children, 1977.

2

Defining Maltreatment

Although throughout human history there have been instances of child maltreatment, it has only been since the 1960s that the phenomenon has been the subject of empirical study. While it is impossible to say with certainty whether the rates of child abuse have changed significantly over generations, current evidence suggests that it is a problem of staggering magnitude. For example, Straus et. al. (1980) point to nearly two million cases of physical abuse each year in the United States alone. Add to that the huge number of children who are sexually abused, neglected, and emotionally traumatized and the figure could reach well over 10 million. Moreover, there is nearly a total absence of studies investigating rates of child abuse world wide.

Obviously, statistical estimates of child maltreatment will vary depending upon how "abuse" is defined. Social workers, physicians and other experts are not in clear agreement as to what constitutes child abuse and neglect. Furthermore, the theorizing of experts and the federal and state laws are so new and untested that they provide for a variety of social, legal and school interpretations and responses.

This variety of responses has important implications for the schools of this country as they seek to do what they can to lessen abuse and neglect and reduce the negative impact on children of past maltreatment. If concerted action in harmony with other social and law enforcement agencies is required of our educators, then it seems that a great deal of shared understanding is essential for all parties concerned. Furthermore, this shared understanding should be reflected in the working policies the schools develop to deal with the problems. At the very least, there should be some measure of agreement in perspectives about the nature of abuse and neglect and about the roles of educators if they are to have adequate coordination of their efforts. Certainly educators and community leaders do not want to be working at cross purposes, and they may well work at cross purposes if they fail to understand and appreciate the legal and professional responsibilities and limitations of all parties involved.

However, given the variety of views about child abuse and neglect, it will not be an easy matter for educators to clearly delineate their roles in regard to abused and neglected students, their students' parents or their colleagues in other community agencies. To compound the problem, there are varying national, state and local laws, regulations and customs on child abuse and neglect to be considered. In addition, there are numerous other legal and social obligations and rights assigned students, parents, educators, schools, social agencies, courts and law enforcement personnel, all of which affect the ability of educators and others to work together to reduce abuse and neglect.

On the other hand, there is an emerging orientation in the laws of this land and among the experts on child abuse and neglect to warrant the development of more effective school policies and programs than has been possible in the past. In this and the following chapter, we discuss certain of these emerging legal, quasi-legal and expert approaches associated with abuse and neglect. From these descriptions we will then proceed to outline suggested policies and programs for schools to consider as they attempt to carry out the mandates of federal and state law.

FEDERAL AND STATE LAWS

Federal Law

The culmination of years of effort by many people was the federal legislation on child abuse passed in 1974. It was a milestone in the movement to provide for the rights of children. On January 31, 1974, the President signed *Public Law 93-247,* a law that said child abuse and neglect is any . . .

physical or mental injury, sexual abuse, negligent treatment or maltreatment of a child under the age of eighteen by a person who is responsible for the child's welfare under circumstances which indicate that the child's health or welfare is harmed or threatened (see *Appendix A*).

This federal definition of child abuse and neglect, however, fails to identify in clear terms what abuse, injury and negligent treatment or maltreatment are—leaving their specification to the courts and other enabling state legislation. At this time, the federal law is essentially untested for constitutional and other legal issues and allows for considerable variation in interpretation. Obviously, this is reflected in the variety of state laws and implementing regulations developed by state agencies. Of course, it is the state law and implementing regulations which the schools need to be most cognizant of at this time.

State Laws

The laws in many states are also vague and untested. And while in some states they are more specific than in others, a great deal of variation in judicial and regulatory response to them occurs. Perhaps it may be helpful to examine certain of these variations among the states.*

Casky (1975, p. 196) illustrated the variation in approaches of various states in a review of the laws of Colorado, Arizona, and Texas. In Colorado, abuse means the child specifically:

> . . . exhibits evidence of skin bruising, bleeding, malnutrition, sexual molestation, burns, fracture of any bone, subdural hematoma, soft tissue swelling, failure to thrive or death, and such condition or death is not justifiably explained, or where the history given concerning such condition or death may not be the product of an accident . . .

In the above Colorado Law, most of the conditions are relatively specific and can be agreed upon. However, the

---

*We have included the child protection laws of Michigan, Ohio and Maine in the appendices as illustrations of what we believe are typical laws regarding reporting, child protection, detainment authority procedures and penalties. The reader should examine legislation on child abuse in his or her own state—copies of which should be available from local child protection agencies.

phrase "failure to thrive" is vague, not easily defined, and will be cause for differences in interpretation. One result may be that many educators will be reluctant about reporting their perceptions of "failure to thrive".

Similarly, the actual determination of malnutrition and when it must be considered the result of abuse or neglect, involves judgement or opinion—even for physicians and judges. However, if one thinks there is a lack of precision in the Colorado definition of child abuse, consider Arizona's:

> (child abuse is) . . . the infliction of physical or mental injury or the causing of deterioration of a child and shall include failing to maintain reasonable care and treatment or exploiting or overworking a child to such an extent that his health, morals, or emotional well-being is endangered (as reported in DeFrancis, 1970, p. 114).

On the other hand, Texas was very precise in its 1974 *Texas Family Code* when it broadened its conception of abuse "with the mandate to report violation of compulsory school attendance laws on three or more occasions" (Casky, 1975). However, precision does not necessarily imply agreement or ease of enforcement. Several educators, social workers and law enforcement persons, when interviewed on this matter by the senior author, indicated that they would be very hesitant to apply the label and stigma of "abusive parent" to anyone whose child had missed only three days of school with that parent's knowledge unless the absences were seen as part of a larger picture involving other conditions of abuse or neglect.

In 1975, the Michigan Legislature, typical of other legislatures, also broadened the concept by specifically distinguishing child abuse from child neglect, but in doing so used many phrases which may be considered in legal appeals and court interpretations. Michigan's 1975 Child Protection Law states:

> "Child abuse" means harm or threatened harm to a child's health or welfare by a person responsible for the child's health or welfare which occurs through non-accidental physical or mental injury, sexual abuse, or maltreatment.

> "Child neglect" means harm to a child's health or welfare by a person responsible for the child's health or welfare which occurs through negligent treatment, including the failure to provide adequate food, clothing, shelter, or medical care.

Clearly, the Colorado and Texas definitions given above were written in more precise language than were the

Arizona and Michigan definitions of child abuse.* In all states, however, there are sources of confusion in the child protection laws which will demand the attention of many segments of society. There are several questions these laws pose for constitutional rights, law enforcement and regulation. Most assuredly, there will be several court suits and legal opinions before there is a reasonable consensus about what child maltreatment is beyond that of the more severe and obvious forms of child battering and neglect.

Our point in emphasizing this diversity in statutes regarding child abuse is that we as educators or community leaders need to be constantly aware of current definitions of child abuse and child neglect in our particular communities. Definitions of maltreatment are not so clearcut, consistent and enforceable as is sometimes suggested. Not only do we need to be aware of the current laws, regulations and opinions in our own states but we must be particularly aware of the fact that acceptable definitions are yet to emerge in court decisions, the views of experts and the opinions of the public.

---

*It is not our intention to argue the merits of specific definitions of abuse and neglect versus more general definitions. They both have merit and present problems.

REGULATIONS OF CHILD PROTECTIVE SERVICES

It is also important to recognize that the law in regard to child abuse is an expression of intent by legislators—that, as a matter of reality, we seldom deal with the law directly. Rather, we work most often with the regulations and actions of regulatory and enforcement agencies designed to implement policies and regulations which will assist in the enforcement of the law. Again we emphasize, as educators, we need to be conscious of what these policies and regulations are in our own particular districts and how we can best work together to implement them. The regulatory agency that is most concerned with child protection services and issues regulations to implement state laws varies from state to state. Every educator should know the name of the child protective services agency in his or her state and school district. From them, they should acquire the regulations for school involvement in child maltreatment cases.

Of course, the regulations of child protective service agencies, like all other governmental regulatory bodies, are subject to emerging court decisions. For example, the authors know of one state where the regulations of the child protective service agency regarding record keeping—designed to curb child abuse—are being considered at this time for challenge in court as an infringement on citizenship rights. Some believe that their particular regulations are in violation of constitutional rights to privacy. Whatever the eventual legal outcome, the situation is fluid and will probably remain so for several years. But even so, the orders of regulatory agencies, including those of child protective services, usually carry the weight of law until changed by court or legislative acts. It is important for educators to be aware that the regulations of child protective services carry the force of the law. They will be in a position to then communicate information back to their school staff regarding regulations, enforcement and other important considerations.

Since neither laws nor regulations are likely to be equally enforced, the school staff should be able to find out through liaison personnel what law enforcement and social agency personnel in their area are stressing, the regulations and laws that are being ignored, along with the reasons for such practices. For example, in some communities there is reluctance among social workers to always involve the police when a crime has been committed by parents against their children. This is especially true when social workers believe that police involvement may cause more child abuse. One conclusion is that if we wish to understand the current "operating" definitions of child abuse and neglect laws, we need to look closely at what the social agencies responsible for treatment in our districts are saying to us as educators. This means, of course, going beyond the rhetoric and polemics which characterize so much of the communications put out for public consumption.

SUGGESTED READINGS

Bourne, Richard, and Newberger, Eli H. (Editors), CRITI-CAL PERSPECTIVES ON CHILD ABUSE. Lexington, MA: Lexington Books, 1979.

Clements, T. J., CHILD ABUSE: THE PROBLEM OF DEFINITION. Creighton Law Review, Vol. 8, No. 4, 729-742, June, 1975.

Garbarino, James and Gillian, Gwen, UNDERSTANDING ABUSIVE FAMILIES, Lexington, MA: Lexington Books, 1980.

Kamerman, S. B. and Harte, A., CHILD ABUSE AND NEGLECT: PROBLEMS, POLICIES, NAD PROVI-SION. Columbia University, School of Social Work, New York, Report No. 3, 1975.

Mayer, Adele, INCEST. Holmes Beach, FL: Learning Publications, 1983.

Pelton, Leroy, THE SOCIAL CONTEXT OF CHILD ABUSE AND NEGLECT. New York: Human Services Press, 1981.

Straus, Murray A., Gelles, Richard J., Steinmetz, Suzanne K., BEHIND CLOSED DOORS: VIOLENCE IN THE FAMILY. Garden City, NY: Anchor Press/Double-day, 1980.

Talan, T., DeFrank, C. and Gamm, S., CHILD ABUSE AND NEGLECT LEGAL HANDBOOK. Child Advocate Association, 1978.

U.S. Department of Health, Education and Welfare, INTERDISCIPLINARY GLOSSARY ON CHILD ABUSE AND NEGLECT: LEGAL, MEDICAL, SO-CIAL WORK TERMS. (OHDS) 78-30137, February 1, 1978.

3

Understanding Parents

Battered children have made "good" news copy for newspapers and other media for a number of years and we should be thankful for this coverage. Articles and books about the battered child have helped us to become more aware of our responsibilities. Clearly we owe a great debt to such early writers as Vincent J. Fontana, Ray E. Helfer, C. Henry Kempe, David Gil, Vincent De Francis and others too numerous to mention, for activating the public, professionals and their legislators.

On the other hand, as a result of the emphasis on the battered child in the public media, we have been left with many problems. Child abuse, as we have noted, includes far more children than those who have been tortured, maimed, or otherwise battered. The problem of child abuse also includes parents who do not inflict grim physical beatings. Just as Kempe and Helfer (1972) recognized when they indicated that it was time to expand the definition of the abused child, we need to expand our understanding of abusive parents. We also need to expand our understanding of the social forces affecting abuse as exemplified in the work of Straus et al. (1980) and Garbarino and Gillian (1980).

THE NEED TO BE INFORMED

Unfortunately, as a result of the emphasis on "battering" parents and traditions of retribution, too many people still respond to instances of reported child abuse as simply being cases where the courts, law enforcement organizations and social welfare agencies should remove children and punish parents. While such a view may be appropriate on occasion, it may be more harmful than helpful to a very large proportion of our abused children.

Dr. C. Henry Kempe, one of the leading authorities on child abuse, indicates that only about ten percent of the abused children would be better off removed from their parents. Dr. Kempe estimates that with considerable support from trained and capable specialists, ninety percent of the abusive parents can be helped to provide nonabusive and healthy homes for their children (Shanas, 1975).

We believe that if educators learn to understand some of the family dynamics associated with both extreme and mild forms of child abuse and neglect, it will help them in their relationships with both abused children and children from healthy family situations. With an understanding of the sufferings and effects of child maltreatment, they will be able to more effectively teach, counsel and otherwise provide assistance to all students. In addition, learning about the dynamics of family relations, particularly in regard to child maltreatment, will help educators in their inevitable relationships with parents through conferences, communications sent home and other school-parent activities.

We are quite aware that schools have no legal responsibility to insist that parents provide particular kinds of child training or other living arrangements.* By and large, our schools are legally charged to structure arrangements at school for students. As far as abuse or neglect by parents is concerned, educators are supposed to report their suspicions and provide help in substantiation. In nearly every state, treatment of the family in a child abuse or neglect case is to be turned over to legally approved agencies who are authorized to work with parents. However, it would be naive to think that through such legal divisions of labor and authority educators can be left out of the picture, even if so desired.

The schools have been charged by both federal and state law to provide for all children, including those who

---

*Of course, schools can legally insist, as a prerequisite for school attendance, that students be living in the school district with parents or approved adults.

are socially and psychologically in need of special assistance. The schools cannot effectively meet that charge unless they have access to considerable information and support from outside the classroom. Likewise, educators should do all they can to assist service agencies and volunteers by providing information and support with respect to each case.

Everywhere, in recognition of the need for educators to work with parents, federal and state regulations and laws have been written specifically to involve parents and educators in mutual activities. The *Title I* of *ESEA* and its regulations regarding the teaching of disadvantaged children and the federal law on mainstreaming exceptional children (PL 94-142) are but two of the recent legal demands which specifically include statements recognizing that parents must be involved in educational decisions. Furthermore, if we have learned anything through our efforts to understand behavior and learning in school, it is that we should take into account the skills, values and health of particular students, as well as conditions of their nurturance, if we are to maximize our effectiveness. Educators have a professional need to know a great deal about the lives of all of their students if they are to fully help them. This does not mean that they need to know or should know everything. What they should know about abuse and neglect and how they should learn what they need to know is one concern of this book.

We should also recognize that as educators we have a role to play with parents whether we want to or not. For example, how teachers interact with students on the playground, in the gym, in the classroom, the assignments they make, the substance of what they intentionally or unintentionally teach about society, their placements of students in varying school activities and the formal and informal labels they apply to children and to others in society combine to affect the interactions between students and their parents.

The same is true for the many types of interactions teachers have with parents. In teacher conferences, what otherwise may be considered appropriate information to be given parents in order to help students in school could, in fact, make matters worse. Most assuredly, if this is true in the case of parents who are not legally abusive to their children, it is most certainly true for parents who are abusive. Teachers are considerably affected by the judgements of their student's parents and *vice versa*. We are all affected in what we do in responding to others by our judgements of them. Therefore, it is very appropriate for us as educators to be accurate in assessing all of the pertinent contingencies which impinge on our students' development and learning — and some of the most pertinent contingencies impinging on student development and learning in our classrooms are events occurring in our students' homes.

STEREOTYPES OF ABUSIVE PARENTS

To be sure, the family provides a large part of the experience which determines the child's condition in the school setting and *vice versa.* In this regard, we need to learn that being labeled an abusive parent—either informally or formally—tells us very little indeed about what such parents are like or what they are doing. Furthermore, being labeled an "abusive parent" is a very risky thing because it may have the unintended consequence of activating false stereotypes which impede our helping those we are legally charged to assist.

Regretably, much of the literature on abusive parents tends to create stereotypes. At this point, the professional literature relies heavily on official records and a few studies with serious methodological limitations.* We have observed

---

*We do not intend to suggest that past research studies on child abuse have been so poor that they should not have been conducted or reported. Rather, we believe that research on characteristics of abusive parents is just beginning, that much is to be learned; that those who conducted and/or reported the early studies have provided a real service in making the public sensitive. We believe, however, that the research to date is just that—a beginning—and does not definitely characterize the problem or provide answers we should hold with great confidence.

that far too seldom do the articles in the professional literature of social work, education, sociology and psychology,
when dealing with this subject, criticially evaluate the research designs which have produced many of the statements
stereotyping abusive parents.

This is one reason why it is important to involve trained
and experienced child protective service workers at the
point of any suspicions an educator may have regarding
the family. The professional child protection worker, if
properly trained, experienced and supported, can provide
educators with a much clearer and more detailed understanding than one can ever gain from reading the thousands
of lists circulated in the public media and professional
literature by well-intentioned lay and professional persons.

Even so, the enumeration of characteristics of abusive
parents seems to be expanding and clearly suggests that
abusive and/or neglective parents are not all alike. This,
in turn, suggests that identification and intervention strategies should take into account this expanding awareness.

CHARACTERISTICS OF ABUSIVE PARENTS

The fact that abusive parents are not all alike can be
seen in the variety of characteristics included in lists being
circulated to educators and others. It is particularly important as we review these lists that we be careful not to

exhibit class or ethnic ethnocentrism. Such prejudices and stereotypes often function to obscure rather than clarify the issue. To be sure, certain categories of abuse and neglect may be more easily observed in one social class than another. However, such observations should not be the basis of class bias. To restate our point, child abuse is a pervasive phenomenon throughout our culture, such that it is not limited to racial, ethnic, or socioeconomic groupings.

Many abusive parents, however, seem to share certain characteristics. For example, many parents who abuse their children:

- Have been abused by their parents when they were themselves children;

- Are often judged by mental health workers as "socially" and "psychologically" immature;

- See themselves as inadequate and worthless and are unwilling to recognize that their child is dependent on them;

- Are easily hurt by real or imagined criticism or rejection from their children;

- View the child as a small adult, capable of meeting their needs when the child, in fact, lacks such capability;

- Experience exaggerated frustration as a result of their perception of the children's failure;

- Act out their frustrations through impulsive violence against their child; have learned to be violent against children when they were abused themselves as children;

- Hold unrealiztic behavioral expectations for their children, often reflecting lack of awareness of typical stages of cognitive and physical development among children;

- Are abusing alcohol or drugs; and/or

- Are experiencing violence in the marital relationship.

CHARACTERISTICS OF NEGLECTING PARENTS

Similar to the list above for abusing parents, neglecting parents sometimes are characterized as exhibiting:

- Inability to tolerate stress or frustration;

- Inability to express anger directly and deal with anger by sulking;

- Have a desire to be rid of the demands of their children;

- Show an indifference toward being a parent; and/or

- Display little in the ways of parental planning.

Obviously, the above characteristics are psychological traits which may or may not predispose parents to engage in abuse or neglect. No attempt is made here to assess the validity of these lists of psychological conditions of abusive and neglecting parents, nor are any discussions presented in the literature about social conditions such as unemployment, family strife, etc. which may produce these conditions. Our intention here is merely to alert the reader to current common explanations and suggest that researchers in the future may have much more to say about the factors which contribute to child abuse and neglect.

THE NEED FOR CAUTION

One difficulty with employing lists such as the above in in-service training sessions for educators without considerable critique and elaboration is that they can lead to over-simplified and perhaps even distorted views of the problem, what to look for and how to respond. Statements that may be relatively true in themselves can lead to very distorted perceptions and implications.

For example, take another area where a similar problem occurs—that of alcoholism. It is commonly cited that alcoholics are likely to come from families with one or two alcoholic parents. This is relatively true in terms of incidence. What is not commonly reported, and equally true, is that the second highest incidence rate is for alcoholics to come from families where alcohol is strictly forbidden (Ackerman, 1983). In only learning one of the two correct statements about the family backgrounds of alcoholics, one may well overlook important conditions affecting alcoholism. Also, there are a lot of alcoholics who come from families at every level of drinking.

We can come to a similar conclusion about parents who are abusive to their children. To be sure, many abusive parents were abused when they were children. In terms of the available research, we find no particular fault with Helfer and Kempe (1972) when they state: "For abuse to occur, the parent must be predisposed, *often* as the result of his or her own personal history, to use violent childrearing techniques and mechanisms." We also find little fault with Forrer's statement that: "*Many* child beaters have themselves suffered battering as a child and rely on these abusive techniques in dealing with their own children" (Forrer, 1973). However, there is considerable data and writing to suggest that there are many abusive parents who were not physically abused or neglected when they were children. We suspect that not every abused child becomes an abusive parent anymore than we believe that all children of alcoholics become alcoholics themselves—they do not. It is our view that no *single* variable in a person's past or present circumstances is sufficient to produce abusive tendencies. Rather, it is the complex interaction of numerous variables that can lead to child abuse or neglect.

The implications of our observations for educators and service agency personnel will be discussed in subsequent chapters. Given the inadequacy of research to date, it is crucial that when a child is suspected of being abused or neglected, a trained person who has learned more than the stereotypes *from stereotypical biases* visit and study the home conditions. There is no adequate substitute for training and experience to be found in the literature, especially when it comes to diagnosing a particular child and his or her parents. It is for this reason that educators must have access to well-trained professionals from protective service agencies and that these professionals be in frequent communication with educators concerning developments in each case.

SUGGESTED READINGS

Ackerman, Robert, CHILDREN OF ALCOHOLICS, 2nd
Ed. Holmes Beach, FL: Learning Publications, Inc.,
1983.

Education Commission of the States, TEACHER EDUCA-
TION—AN ACTIVE PARTICIPANT IN SOLVING
THE PROBLEM OF CHILD ABUSE AND NEGLECT.
Child Abuse Project, Denver, Colorado, Report No. 99,
April, 1977.

Harmon, David and Brin, Jr., Orville G., LEARNING TO
BE PARENTS: PRINCIPLES, PROGRAMS, AND
METHODS. Beverly Hills, CA: Sage Publications, 1980.

Kempe, C. H., "Arresting or Freezing the Developmental
Process: Related Aspects in Psychiatry." In: R. E. Hel-
fer and C. H. Kempe (Eds.), CHILD ABUSE AND
NEGLECT. THE FAMILY AND THE COMMUNITY.
Cambridge, Massachusetts: Ballinger Publishing Co.,
1976.

Kadushin, Alfred, and Martin, Judith, CHILD ABUSE:
    AN INTERACTIONAL EVENT. New York: Columbia
    University Press, 1981.

Martin, J. P. (Editor), VIOLENCE AND THE FAMILY.
    New York: John Wiley and Sons, 1978.

Mayer, Adele, INCEST. Holmes Beach, FL: Learning Pub-
    lications, Inc., 1983.

4

Incest: A Special Case

Of all forms of child maltreatment, incest seems to generate the greatest controversy, confusion and debate. Experts and lay persons alike express disagreement concerning the seriousness of the problem, the reasons for incest, the degree of harm done, and the effectiveness of legislative and human service programs. Further compounding the controversy is a shroud of myth and a general dearth of empirical research into the phenomenon. However the efforts of women's groups, child rights advocates, social workers, educators, medical professionals and others have called attention to the serious problem that demands a coordinated response. This chapter will examine the range of child sexual abuse patterns and offer practical strategies to enable effective intervention.

DIMENSIONS OF THE PROBLEM

Child abuse in general, and sexual abuse in particular, engender such intense feelings of moral outrage that impartial analysis often is problematic. Although there is

considerable cross cultural variation in social norms regarding childhood sexuality, in most Western societies
there are stringent avoidance taboos concerning many
types of child-adult interactions. Depending upon who is
rendering judgment, definitions of sexual abuse can include everything from verbal discussions of human sexuality with children, to overt acts of exhibitionism, molestation and rape. According to the Federal Child Abuse
Prevention and Treatment Act of 1974, sexual abuse of
children is defined as follows:

> . . . the obscene or pornographic photographing,
> filming or depiction of children for commercial pur-
> poses, or the rape, molestation, ncest, prostitution
> or other such forms of sexual exploitation of chil-
> dren under circumstances which indicate that the
> child's health or welfare is harmed or threatened . . .

While legal definitions help sensitize one to the problem, there is still dispute as to the exact meaning of behavior such as incest or at what point a child's health is
threatened. Given the difficulty in defining the problem,
it is little wonder that statistics indicating the incidence
of sexual abuse exhibit considerable variation. For example,
in the United States estimates of incest, the most common
type of sexual abuse, vary between 200,000 to over 10
million cases per year (Mayer, 1983). Kinsey's (1953) clas-
sic research claimed that 24 percent of all females are
molested during childhood, though he questions the degree
of actual harm this poses. Added to these figures are

estimates of several hundred thousand adolescents involved with prostitution each year, often as a result of running away from a family where they were abused. While it is impossible to determine with certitude the exact number of sexual abuse cases, consensus is growing that there exists a problem of staggering magnitude.

The changing status of the family should also be recognized. For example, the percentage of stepfathers and live-in male friends, who play a disportionate role in sexual abuse and incest is likely to increase. In reflecting on the changing family patterns that characterize our society today, by 1990 it is projected that 50% of all children will have lived part of their first 18 years in a single parent family or reconstituted family. We will need to give more attention to the potential increase in sexual abuse among non-biologically related family members.

PATTERNS OF SEXUAL VICTIMIZATION

Stereotypes of "dirty old men" and "perverted wierdoes" stalking children at parks and playgrounds are inaccurate representations of most offenders. Evidence consistently shows that the overwhelming majority of sexual abuse cases occur within the family. In only about 3 to 10 percent of the cases are the perpetrators total strangers to the victims (Luther and Price, 1980). Father-daughter or stepfather-daughter relationships are by far the most common, accounting for 70 to 80 percent of reported sexual abuse cases (Goodwin, 1982). Mother-son or mother-daughter sexual relationships are relatively uncommon.

The "typical" victim of sexual abuse is female, between ages 8 to 12, who endures a pattern of sexual victimization over a prolonged period of time (rather than a single episode), and usually is a relative or close acquaintance of the perpetrator (Finklehor, 1979). Although penetration does occur in a percentage of cases (usually with older victims), the relationship more frequently involves fondling, oral-genital stimulation, and/or exhibitionism. Physical violence is seldom used to force children into sexual activity, though a combination of threat, deception and/or promise of reward is common. There are at least two basic reasons for this general absence of physical force:

1. The adult needs the cooperation of the victim in terms of   the child remaining silent and an available partner for an extended period of time. To physically hurt the child would diminish the chances of such cooperation and increase the likelihood of discovery.

2. Children are susceptible to an adult's position of physical, material, and presumably moral dominance. The child's loyalty, trust, and dependence on adults are used against the child to draw him or her into sexual activity.

In addition, fear of family disintegration is often cited as a motive for the child's cooperation with an adult family member. However, it is our view that such fear is usually a reason for the child's failure to divulge the abuse, rather than the initial reason for becoming involved in the liaison. We do not wish to imply that the victim consents to, or is responsible for, sexual involvement with the adult. Indeed, we reject the psychoanalytic and other traditions which suggest, without empirical evidence, that children often instigate incestuous liaisons with adults.

As in the case of rape, there are stereotypes and, in our view, false assumptions concerning the degree of victim-precipitation of the experience. Some have asserted that the child victim is being "seductive" or is spontaneously acting out "oedipal-electra" fantasies, or enjoys the "special attention" and therefore bears at least partial responsibility. For example, in a widely cited article, Kaufman et. al. (1954) claims that daughters welcome the sexual advances of their fathers as an indication of parental love. Although one could debate the issue of whether sexual abuse of children is the legal, moral, and psychological equivalent of rape, we fundamentally agree with those who argue that children, by definition, *cannot* give consent to engage in sexual practices with adults. As Mayer states (1983: 14), "Adult offenders ultimately bear responsibility for incestuous abuse. It is they who, at the expense of their victims, act out sexually with all the power that their adult and parental roles convey."

Yet another popular though untested belief places considerable responsibility on the mother for father-daughter incest. Kaufman et. al., (1954) talk in psychoanalytic terms about the mother's "unconscious desire" to place the daughter in the maternal role, thus relieving herself of the responsibilities of wife and lover. Thus it is argued that the mother actually pushes the father and daughter into a sexual relationship by abandoning her responsibilities as wife and mother. Henderson (1972) represents this view as follows:

> Most authors agree that the father is aided and abetted in his incestuous liaison by a collusive wife . . . She forces a heavy burden of responsibility on to her daughter by causing her to assume the role of wife and lover with her own father [thus]absolving the mother of this unwanted role.

We strongly reject the notion that either the mother or the daughter, consciously or unconsciously, is responsible for encouraging the father to enter into an incestuous relationship. Not only does such an untested theory carry sexist overtones, but it functions to compound the problem of helping victims and their families. While it is true that incest may be indicative of general family dysfunction, victims are not the cause of this dysfunction. Likewise it may be true that in some cases mothers suspect an incestuous relationship between father and daughter but, for a variety of reasons (e.g., feared loss of economic support), fail to act upon this suspicion. A child's understanding of sexuality differs from the perceptions and motivations of adults. In order to effectively respond to the needs of children and other family members, it is important to understand the family dynamics involved and the consequences of sexual abuse.

FAMILY DYNAMICS

Although theories concerning the causes of child sexual abuse abound, the problem is multifaceted and hence no single explanation is sufficient to account for all cases. In truth, there is considerable variation between offenders, victims, and family interaction patterns, as well as intervention strategies. However there are certain family dynamics operating that are relatively common to many abuse situations.

Similar to the general pattern of physical abuse cases, social isolation is frequently cited as a factor in sexual abuse. Social isolation is not necessarily a function of geographic location, but rather is determined by the number and quality of relationships outside the family. A lack of external outlets can result in the development of sexual involvements within the family, as well as insulate such actions from the scrutiny of outsiders. Given the lack of an external support system, there tends to be a heavy dependence on family members to meet emotional and sexual needs. Typically it is not a pedophilic craving for children that leads to an incestuous relationship with one's off-spring. Rather, it is this near total dependence, perhaps coupled with an unwillingness to seek exogamous sexual contact, that appears to be crucial; and once a pattern of incest begins, a feared stigma of public disclosure tends to further isolate the family.

The occurrence of incest is both symptomatic of, and a catalyst for, family stress or dysfunction. Marital discord and sexual incompatibility between husband and wife, economic difficulties, illness, prolonged absence followed by the return of the father, fear of abandonment or family disintegration, death of spouse, and role conflict have all been cited as possible reasons for incest. At the very least, the presence of incest indicates that familial role relation-ships are disorganized, with considerable conflict encom-passing parent-child roles. Contrary to popular belief how-ever, there is little evidence to suggest that parental mental illness or "psychopathology" is a causal factor in the sexual abuse of children. Nevertheless the confusion over role expectations, fear, shame, guilt and low self-esteem associa-ted with incest typically add considerable emotional stress to victims, offenders, and other family members.

Another common factor in father-daughter incest is al-cohol abuse (DHHS, 1981). As many as 50% of reported cases involve an alcoholic father (Goodwin, 1982). As in the case of physical abuse, we do not believe that alcohol "causes" the behavior, it merely provides a convenient excuse or face-saving rationalization for the conduct. However unlike most physical abuse, sexual abuse differs in two important respects. First, sexual abuse tends to be *premeditated,* not a spontaneous act carried out in a state of rage. Second, whereas there are norms that support hitting a child in the name of discipline, there are no norms which call for sexual relations between parent and child. Little wonder that offenders may contemplate suicide upon disclosure. However both physical and sexual abuse tend to occur over an extended period of time (months or years) and may involve more than one child.

IMPACT ON VICTIMS AND FAMILIES

There is considerable controversy surrounding the issue of whether or not children are harmed by sexual contact with adults. Some argue that the "innocence of childhood" functions as a natural protection against traumatic life events experienced in the early years. In addition, because children have only a vague comprehension of the social norms regulating sexuality, they neither perceive nor are traumatized by the violation of sexual taboos. Shultz (1980) argues that only 5 to 10 percent of sexual abuse cases involve physical injury. In the remainder of the cases, he argues, there is little evidence to support the belief that incest results in long-term psychological damage. Likewise, Kinsey (1953, p. 121) states that "it is difficult to understand why a child, except for its cultural conditioning, should be disturbed at having its genitals touched, or disturbed at seeing the genitalia of other persons."

Critics of this view claim that incest victims suffer deep emotional trauma that endures into adulthood. Some equate the psychological consequences of incest with those of rape. Many mental health professionals point to the confusion, fear, shame, low self-esteem and thoughts of suicide among large numbers of victims as evidence of trauma. Several studies indicate that a significant percentage of women who undergo psychiatric treatment report a history of being sexually abused during childhood (Finklehor, 1979). Accordingly, the Department of Health and Human Services states the following (1981, p. 6):

> The fact that many women reveal their incestuous history while involved in therapy for other problems, suggests that the damage from child sexual abuse may be related to other problems for which they are seeking help. Depression and confusion about their own identities are common reactions of many victims. Some jump into early marriages as a means of escaping their family situations and dealing with their feelings of aloneness. Some report feeling "marked" or stigmatized for life . . .

To be sure, variables such as age of victim, frequency of occurrence, degree of physical force, relationship to offender, etc. are key factors in attempting to assess the amount of harm done to victims. While not all children are affected to the same degree, we believe that there are sufficiently large numbers of victims who are traumatized by incest and thus we strongly reject the argument that it causes no harm. Many juveniles who run away from home, many youth involved in delinquency, large numbers of prostitutes, and many who require the care of therapists or otherwise behave in nonadaptive ways have experienced sexual abuse. Given the deleterious consequences of sexual abuse, it is of paramount importance for educators and others in contact with children and adolescents to recognize the symptoms and understand the do's and don'ts of effective intervention and support.

SUGGESTED READINGS

Luther, S.L.; Price, J.H., "Child sexual abuse: a review." *Journal of School Health* 50(3): 161-165, March, 1980.

Thorman, George, INCESTUOUS FAMILIES. Springfield, IL: Charles C. Thomas, 1983.

Part B
The School and
Protective Services

5

Developing
School Policies

The development of school policy guidelines dealing with child abuse and neglect at the district and building level is an important step in combating the problem. Perhaps more than any other group, school staff have a unique opportunity to observe and report on child maltreatment as well as to facilitate preventive and remediation programs. If this opportunity is to be capitalized upon, it is imperative that each school district formulate written policies to guide their school personnel in the details of what they can and should do regarding child neglect and abuse. Certainly, as some have contended, failure to establish policies may inadvertantly commit the schools to inaction. Furthermore, specific procedures and staff responsibilities must be spelled out in detail and communicated to teachers, school counselors, administrators, etc., throughout the various levels of the school system if efforts aimed at prevention and treatment are to achieve maximum success.

Policies on child abuse and neglect are critical. However, we might add that policies which are not *implemented*
are of little use and may be worse than no policy at all.
This is especially true if such policies communicate the
idea that action is being taken yet there is no real change
in outcome. Responses to the problem should be more
than symbolic. As every thoughtful person knows, many
excellent policies can be sabotaged, misunderstood, or
simply ignored. It is often very easy for an administrator
to create the illusion of action by formulating a policy;
yet, we all know that an equally important task is to elicit
the system-wide cooperation needed to insure the implementation of such a policy. In this vein, we would like to
suggest strategies for developing policy guidelines, as well
as to consider what might be the substance of effective
school policies.

The first step is for those on the staff who recognize
the importance of dealing with child maltreatment to get
together and discuss two broad areas of concern: 1) how to
achieve a workable policy; and 2) the important elements
that the eventual policy might include. The final outcome
may emerge as something not anticipated, but uniting
people who have a genuine interest in the problem—not
just those who are directed to be involved—is crucial to
effective policy implementation. Of course, many people
still must be convinced of the need for a policy.

Unfortunately, according to the Education Commission of the States (1976), only 44% of the largest school districts in each of the fifty states had adopted written policies on child abuse as of 1975. "The very poor record of schools as reporting agents is testimony to this (Garbarino and Gillian, 1980). Of the smallest districts in each state, only 29% had formal operational policies in the area of child abuse and neglect. Likewise, Drews (1972) reports that while 49% of administrators answering a questionnaire indicated that their system had some type of standard operating procedure, only 24% of the principals, teachers and school nurses were aware of such a procedure. This suggests the need for educators to become involved in forming policies, communicating these policies throughout the system and fostering cooperation in implementing these policies.

Although much has been accomplished since these studies alerted us to a problem, the fact remains that many school districts have not yet developed policies on child maltreatment.

POLICY FORMATION AND IMPLEMENTATION*

One of the primary goals of every school district should be to develop a child protection policy that reflects state law and causes school personnel to actively, not passively, try to carry out the spirit of that law. This

---

*See *Appendix B* for an illustration of a sample school policy.

policy should be formulated in such a way that it can be readily implemented at all levels in the school organization. Likewise, this policy must be developed in a manner that facilitates the cooperation of other service agencies in the community. Given that unilateral action tends to meet with relatively little success, it is important to establish an interorganizational network composed of school staff and service agency personnel. The problems of child abuse and neglect are so complex that neither the schools nor social service organizations can effectively deal with them unless they collaborate to form policies, share resources and foster implementation. Maximum community involvement is essential if child abuse and neglect policies are to have the desired effect.

Developing Community Involvement

A first step for interested educators, therefore, is to elicit the support of community professionals, service groups and volunteers in the formation of *ad hoc* committees designed to write school policy in a number of areas, (e.g., identification, reporting, prevention, treatment, etc.).

Schools need to coordinate their efforts in developing school policies with all relevant community organizations, especially in the areas of referral and follow-up, in order to insure efficient and effective handling of each case.

Such collaboration between school and community should begin at the policy formation stage and be maintained throughout the various phases of implementation. Despite the importance of school-community cooperation in the formation of child abuse policy, comparatively few school districts have made much progress in this area.

Of course, such a task is easier said than done. All too often interdisciplinary mistrust, professional pride, and jealousy inhibit various professional groups from working together toward the solution of a common problem. Professionals in one organization may cultivate such a strong sense of pride that they ignore the potential contributions of persons in other organizations. This can even occur within an organization where individuals at different levels protect their "turf" regardless of the needs or goals of the larger system.

Interdisciplinary cooperation may also be inhibited because each group has a somewhat different set of concerns in relation to the overall problem of child protection (e.g., medical, educational, rehabilitative, etc.). Such divergent interests and professional rivalries may lead to a duplication of services, poor communication, poor leadership and a lack of cooperation between the schools and community agencies. The final result may be that even when a policy is created, it is never fully implemented.

There are a number of strategies schools can employ to avoid these difficulties. If the parochial concerns of divergent groups are not to supercede the common goal of insuring the welfare of children, then each group must be made to feel it has a personal and professional stake in achieving such a goal. The best way to accomplish this is to make sure that the different agencies, professional groups and others at each level of the child protective network have input during the policy-making phase. Oftentimes, those who are expected to carry out a policy will feel no vested interest or enthusiasm for doing so *unless* they have formal input in the creation of that policy. Groups at various levels, not just administrators, should help to determine legitimate problems and strategies for collective action. Thus, it is very important for each school district to solicit ideas and feedback from all those who will be involved in the day-to-day implementation of the child protective policy. Involving such a broad constituency in the formation of policy tends to break down the fragmentation between groups and promote a feeling of personal accountability and pride in the overall success of the program. The greater the input from various sectors in the network, the less potential for apathy or opposition to the program.

Developing Task Forces

Given the need to break down the isolation between diverse elements in the school system and community, the central administration of each school district should assume responsibility for establishing a number of task force committees composed of representatives from all the different groups involved in child protection (e.g., law, medicine, social work, education, etc.). The purpose of these task force committees is to make policy recommendations in specific areas of child care which include reporting, follow-up, prevention, therapy, parent education and suggestions to schools.

Fostering Leadership Skills

Perhaps the superintendent of schools, because of his or her leadership skills, influential position and ability to direct resources, should be the one to organize the formation of such interdisciplinary task force committees. However, this should be done with the assistance of those who already have a legal mandate to insure the welfare of children. Optimum size for a working group seems to be five to eight members. Care should be taken to avoid forming committees dominated by one professional area (e.g., medicine, counseling, elementary teaching, social work, etc.). In addition, community volunteer groups and persons should be included at the slightest indication of interest.

Providing Necessary Resources

In order to assist the task forces in carrying out their duties, the central administration, in conjunction with child protection agencies in each district, should provide a number of supportive services to committee members. For example, copies of state statutes on child abuse and neglect should be compiled in advance and distributed to each person serving on a committee. Fact sheets on the incidence of child abuse and neglect in the community as well as lists of resource persons willing to serve as consultants or volunteers could also be assembled. Providing the committees with secretarial assistance and a place where materials can be typed and printed would also be of great help. Such services can be of incalculable value to the successful functioning of the task forces and committees.

The importance of cooperative involvements with community, state and federal public and private agencies will be recognized in the development of resources. Child protective agencies will have available brochures, literature, films and may even arrange for expert speakers on various topics of child abuse and neglect. In the appendices, we provide a listing of resource agencies and a bibliography of materials you may want to consider. However, you should not fail to make best use of the many people and agencies already available in your community who will want to be of assistance.

Creating a Coordinating Council

In addition to forming a series of interdisciplinary committees designed to make policy recommendations in specific areas of child protection, the central administration should create a coordinating council composed of representatives from the school system and all the appropriate child service groups in the community. This coordinating council should receive recommendations from the various committees and assume responsibility for the actual writing of a school system-wide policy. Such a council, in collaboration with the school district administration, should be responsible for integrating the manifold activities of the diverse task forces.

Although the coordinating council represents a centralized policy-making body, its functioning is actually based upon the decentralized operations of constituents throughout all levels of the system. Ideally, this arrangement should enhance inter-agency communication, efficient service utilization and greater participation in carrying out the policy. Once again, the ultimate goal is to write a child protection policy that can be readily implemented in schools and other agencies in the community.

Avoiding the Use of Threat

It is important to stress that the policy should not be perceived as being imposed on school staff from above.

Simply the appearance of an autocratic approach to policy implementation can sometimes alienate those whose support is crucial. Rather, the policy should be seen as emerging from the collaborative efforts of school building staff, central administrative and consultant personnel and community persons, with the central administration merely coordinating these efforts. Such an arrangement has the greatest chance of promoting accountability among all involved. If people feel that they meaningfully participated in creating a policy, they are more likely to take pride and an interest in guaranteeing the successful implementation of that policy.

It is also essential that those at all levels of the school system (e.g., administrators, teachers, counselors, social workers, etc.) and those from outside agencies and volunteers (e.g., child protection agency staff, police, etc.) be encouraged to provide constant feedback regarding successes or difficulties in making the policy work. The policy itself should be constantly evaluated for possible revision in light of this feedback. Administrators should discuss with subordinates potential changes in task directives and provide strong emotional support to encourage involvement. All too often persons in leadership positions vociferously condemn errors in policy execution, thereby stifling necessary feedback from the lower echelons. Generous praise can go a long way toward building the kind of feedback network necessary to achieve maximum policy effectiveness.

Once again, school administrators, the coordinating council and the task forces should solicit policy recommendations from school and community personnel and agencies at all levels and confer praise upon all those who become involved, even if their involvement is minimal. Teachers, teacher-aides, administrators and their organizations (e.g., teachers' unions, counselor organizations, etc.) should all be encouraged to be involved. Such encouragement and support is the best way to foster commitment to the program and enhance the success of child protection efforts.

POLICY COMPONENTS

Formulating a policy should be done in such a way that the policy is not considered to be too fixed or rigid by those who must put it into operation. It is important that a policy on child abuse and neglect be flexible enough to be easily adapted throughout the system. It will also aid in implementation if the policy is divided into a number of specific components.

Presenting a Rationale for Policy

To begin, the policy statement should provide a brief rationale explaining the need for school personnel to become involved in helping to recognize, report, remedy and develop preventive strategies. Included in this rationale should be valid and up-to-date community statistics on child abuse and neglect. A task force should be set up to do a thorough study of the data available and solicit more if needed. This information will be of great value in later evaluations.

The policy statement should also include a discussion of the school's responsibility for the "whole child" with considerable emphasis given to the pedagogical as well as humanitarian reasons for involving educators. Very careful thought should also be given to writing an appeal to educators, an appeal that builds on the educational reasons for the proposed program and stresses the importance of their input and commitment.

Clarifying Legal Obligations

The next step in writing the policy statement is to clarify the statutes and regulations regarding abuse and neglect in the state and nation, but most importantly how they are interpreted in your district. This section should include a discussion of: 1) the federal and state legal definitions of child abuse and neglect, 2) the legal obligations to report suspected cases of abuse and neglect, and 3) the legal immunities from civil or criminal liability for those who report or participate in investigative proceedings. It should be pointed out that most state laws insure confidentiality and protect one for "good faith" reporting. In some cases, failure to report can result in court action. Thus, the statement should indicate possible actions to be taken by the school board for failing to report, as well as state or school board policies regarding confidentiality of report records.

The local agencies who are charged with responsibility for dealing with abuse and neglect (e.g., child protective agencies, court and police) as well as those indirectly involved (e.g., local medical, educational and bar associations) should be especially involved in developing this component of the policy.

Specifying When to Report

In addition to legal aspects, the policy statement should specify the conditions which would justify a report. *Chapters 3* and *6* of this book list symptoms which alert teachers and others to the possibility of physical abuse, sexual abuse, physical neglect and emotional neglect. A task force should decide which of the conditions to include.

It is also imperative that the policy statement specify: 1) the method by which school personnel are to report, 2) the person or persons mandated to file the report, and 3) the person or agency receiving the report. Included here should also be a discussion of the professional ethics of reporting and 4) the person responsible for follow-up.

Building Teams and Coordinators

Included in *Chapter 7* is an illustration of the use of school building child abuse/neglect teams (CAN). The building CAN team (about four staff persons) may include a teacher, nurse, counselor, school social worker, school psychologist or other staff persons who regularly work in the building. The team's coordinator may be the principal or someone appointed by the principal.

Policies should be formulated for the CAN teams regarding:

1. The conduct of interviews and the gathering of data to confirm suspicions of abuse or neglect.

2. The estimation of severity.

3. The receiving and reporting of information where appropriate on abuse and neglect to outside agencies and persons.

4. The facilitating of the school staff in cases of child abuse or neglect.

5. The facilitating of appropriate feedback to school staff regarding outcomes of referrals.

6. The assistance they are to provide in developing workshops, in-service training programs and in distributing materials to facilitate the program.

We believe that building CAN teams are so important that a statement strongly requesting their support should be included in the written policy. In the absence of CAN teams, the principal in each building should be specifically assigned the above tasks in the policy statement.

Specifying Procedures for Reporting

Although classroom teachers, teacher-aides and physical education staff are often in an advantageous position to initially observe suspected cases of abuse and neglect, it is our recommendation that school policies specifically absolve them from the responsibility of actually filing the report. The demands on a teacher's time and energies are great enough without having to fear possible reprisals from parents who may feel threatened. There have actually been

instances of parents threatening or attacking teachers who
have reported children as being possibly maltreated. More
importantly, there may well come a time when the teacher
must work with the parents on educational matters and
thus will need cooperation without undo feelings of ten-
sion. The policy statement should specify that the school
principal, school nurse, or some other school official is
charged with the responsibility of filing the report. However, the policy should clearly state that it is the teacher's
duty (as it is every other school staff person's duty) to
bring his or her observations to the attention of the school
official charged with making the formal report. Following
an oral statement, a written report should be filed. The
next chapter elaborates on suggestions for submitting
reports.

Identifying Community Agencies

Identifying the appropriate agency designated to receive child abuse and neglect cases should be included in
the policy statement (e.g., Child Protective Services). The
functions of the protective service agencies and all other
agencies such as the courts and police should be included
as well. It is necessary that educators be aware of what
agencies can and should do as well as what they cannot do.
It is important that those doing the reporting be clear as
to the lines of authority—who has jurisdiction and when,
who should report to whom, etc.

In an ideal situation, the school would file a report and the appropriate agencies and professionals would respond so as to complement each other. In such a system, problem families would be quickly identified, evaluated and provided with the appropriate services. Unfortunately, this ideal does not always manifest itself. Unless school, agency and professional roles are clearly defined, a number of maladies can occur: duplication of investigations, confusion and struggle over case jurisdiction, cynicism, poor communication between participants, anxiety among family members and perhaps even further danger to the child because of delayed services. Many of these potential problems can be avoided or minimized if the role boundaries of various participants are specified in the policy statement and the channels of communication are clear and remain open.

FORMAT FOR A CHILD ABUSE AND NEGLECT POLICY*

Components	Components to be Cited	Sample Wording
1. Rationale for Policy.	*A brief rationale for involving school personnel in reporting.*	*Because of their sustained contact with school-age children, school employees are in an excellent position to identify abused or neglected children and to refer them for treatment and protection.*
	The name and appropriate section numbers of the state reporting statute.	*To comply with the Mandatory Reporting of Child Abuse or Neglect Act (Sections 3851-3860), Maine Revised Statutes (1975), found in Title 22, Chapter 1056...*
2. Legal Obligations	*Reportable conditions as defined by state law.*	*...who knows or has reasonable cause to suspect that a child has been subjected to abuse or neglect or observes the child being subjected to conditions or circumstances which would reasonably result in abuse...*
	The exact language of the law to define "abuse" and "neglect"; if necessary, explain, clarify or expand.	*"Child abuse and neglect" means physical or mental injury, sexual abuse, negligent treatment or maltreatment of a child under the age of 18 years of age by a person who is responsible for the child's welfare under circumstances which indicate that the child's health or welfare is harmed or threatened thereby.*

*Adapted from:*Child Abuse and Neglect Project, Eduation Commission of the States. Report No. 85 Eduation Policies and Practices Regarding Child Abuse and Neglect and Recommendations for Policy Development.* (April, 1976).

Components	Components to be Cited	Sample Wording
2. Legal Obligations (continued)	*Whether or not there is immunity from civil liability and criminal penalty for those who report or participate in an investigation or judicial proceeding; and whether immunity is for good faith reporting.*	*In Maine, anyone making a report in accordance with the state law or participating in a resulting judicial proceeding is presumed to be acting in good faith and, in doing so, is immune from any civil or criminal liability that might otherwise be imposed.*
	Penalty for failure to report.	*Failure to report may result in a misdemeanor charge: punishment by a fine up to $500.*
	Any provision of the law regarding the confidentiality of records pertaining to reports of suspected abuse or neglect.	*All records concerning reports of suspected abuse or neglect are confidential. Anyone who permits, assists or encourages the release of information from records to a person or agency not legally permitted to have access may be guilty of a misdemeanor.*
3. Professional Obligations	*Who specifically is mandated to report and (if applicable) who may report.*	*. . . it is the policy of the _____ School District that any teacher or other school employee. . .*
	The person or agency to receive reports.	*. . . shall report to the building principal or his or her designated agent who shall then be responsible for making the report to the Department of Human Services. . .*

Components	Components to be Cited	Sample Wording
3. Professional Obligations (Continued)	*The information required of the reporter.*	*. . . and given the following information: names and addresses of the child and his parents or other persons responsible for his care or custody, if known? the child's age, sex and race; the nature and extent of the child's physical injuries, if any; a description of any sexual abuse or neglect to the child or his siblings; family composition; the source of the report, the person making the report; any other information that might help establish the cause of the injuries or condition.*
		School employees shall not contact the child's family or any other persons to determine the cause of the suspected abuse or neglect.
		It is not the responsibility of the school employee to prove that the child has been abused or neglected, or to determine whether the child is in need of protection.
	Expected professional conduct by school employees.	*Any personal interview or physical inspection of the child should be conducted in a professional manner.*
	The method by which school personnel are to report (if appropriate, list telephone number for reporting) and the time in which to report.	*An oral report must be made as soon as possible by telephone or otherwise and may be followed by a written report.*

Components	Components to be Cited	Sample Wording
3. Professional Obligations (Continued)	*Action taken by school board for failure to report.*	*Failure to report may result in disciplinary action against the employee.*

4. Building Teams

   It is the policy of this district to establish in each school a CHILD ABUSE AND NEGLECT TEAM (CAN). This team will consist of _____ members and will have the responsibilities of . . . (See Chapter 6 page 93 for a discussion of CAN teams.)

5. Primary Prevention Policy

   In its child abuse and neglect policy, a school system can specify its role in multidisciplinary cooperation, professional training, public awareness and programs of primary prevention. Although such statements are not necessary, they can help clarify previously ambiguous or ill-conceived positions. The simple process of articulating a clear position can help refocus current porgrams and even allow new program development.

6. Continued Evaluation of Policy

   Policy makers may also find it helpful to articulate a clear policy on evaluation of the school system's child abuse and neglect programs. What are the school system's goals regarding its child abuse and neglect programs? What are the expectations? Are they realistic, measurable? By spelling out realistic expectations and some means to evaluate goals regularly, policy makers can help ensure more effective programs.

A MULTIDISCIPLINARY APPROACH

In conclusion, school and agency officials must keep in mind that the manner in which a policy is developed and the provisions of that policy should reflect a central theme — child abuse and neglect represents a *multidimensional problem* requiring a *multidisciplinary approach* in order to be solved. The collective expertise of relevant community professionals and volunteers should be utilized as a tool for school district administrators and building CAN teams. This multidisciplinary approach that we suggest recognizes the fact that child abuse and neglect is, indeed, a community rather than individual problem, the dimensions of which extend beyond the domain of any single group. The kind of child protection network we advocate can be built upon existing resources in the school district, capable of adapting to community needs, requiring few if any additional funds. By seeking linkages between existing organizations, this team approach will optimize community strengths and establish alliances among those who can provide essential services. In the final analysis, it is our belief that child protection can become a community-wide social movement with troubled families being the ultimate benefactors.

SUGGESTED READINGS

Education Commission of the States, EDUCATION POLI-
CIES AND PRACTICES REGARDING CHILD
ABUSE AND NEGLECT AND RECOMMENDA-
TIONS FOR POLICY DEVELOPMENT. Child Abuse
Project, Denver, Colorado, Report No. 85, April, 1976.

Faller, Kathleen Coulborn, SOCIAL WORK WITH
ABUSED AND NEGLECTED CHILDREN: A
MANUAL OF INTERDISCIPLINARY PRACTICE.
New York: Free Press, 1981.

Gottschalk, B., PERSPECTIVES ON CHILD ABUSE:
A SYNTHETIC APPROACH TO PUBLIC POLICY
MAKING. Master's Thesis, California University,
Berkley, California, June, 1974.

Harriman, R. L., CHILD ABUSE AND THE SCHOOL.
Doctoral Dissertation, University of the Pacific, Stockton, California, 1975.

U.S. Department of Health, Education and Welfare,
MULTIDISCIPLINARY TEAMS IN CHILD ABUSE
AND NEGLECT PROGRAMS. National Center on
Child Abuse and Neglect (DHEW), Publication No.
(OHDS) 78-30152, August, 1978.

6

Identifying
Maltreatment

There are several widely cited lists of conditions for educators to use in detecting parent abuse or neglect. These listings can be found in Ray E. Helfer, *Making the Diagnosis of Child Abuse* (1973), Vincent J. Fontana, *Somewhere a Child is Crying: Maltreatment Causes and Prevention* (1973), and Adele Mayer, *Incest* (1983). These are respected researchers and authors who have done much to alert the public to the problem of child abuse.

In developing their lists of possible indicators of abuse and neglect, Helfer and Fontana refer to several studies, including their own, other experts and several local and state organizations. Among the more influential private and public organizations referred to for work on child abuse and neglect are the American Human Association, the National Committee for the Prevention of Child Abuse and the National Center on Child Abuse and Neglect. These organizations continue to make needed contributions to our society. For years, they have furnished materials on child abuse and neglect to groups and individuals. We urge that every school write to these and other organizations listed in *Appendix G* and *Appendix I*. They will furnish lists to use as guidelines when observing parents and students.

WHEN OBSERVING STUDENTS

Any list should, of course, only be used to sensitize one to the possibility of abuse or neglect. Remember, only a thorough investigation by trained persons will allow for a final determination of abuse or neglect. Obviously, it is crucial that educators be aware of the signs of child maltreatment, because today's children have more contact with school staff than with most groups of adults outside the immediate family. Changing patterns of family living— the demise of the extended family and the increasing incidence of single-parent families—have had the effect of isolating many children from caring adults. Consequently, teachers and other school staff are often among the only adults standing between maltreated children and their abusive or neglecting parents. This clearly suggests that one part of the educator's role is to be able to effectively identify and report suspected cases of abuse or neglect. When we as educators are alert to the signs of child abuse and neglect, we become indispensable allies in preventing and/or eliminating the problem.

Just as educators must be cautious when attempting to construct a profile of abusive parents, so too should we be cautious when drawing a composite of behaviors exhibited by abused children. Much of the literature on child abuse and neglect suggests that there are a number of behavioral signs exhibited by abused children which should immediately alert the educator to the possibility of maltreatment.

While many of these behaviors are indeed correlates of abuse or neglect, children who are not mistreated may also exhibit similar patterns. Likewise, there are students who do not exhibit any particularly alarming emotional or behavioral signs, yet they are also victims of parental abuse. The behavior of abused or neglected children may or may not appear to be "deviant" and may or may not capture the immediate attention of teachers and other school personnel.

Therefore, again we wish to stress: no conclusions should be drawn about a possible case of abuse or neglect until it has been fully investigated by trained persons legally mandated to conduct such investigations. We need to avoid generating false stereotypes or drawing false conclusions about a child's behavior. Nevertheless, there are several maladaptive behavioral signs displayed by children which may be caused by parental mistreatment or by other disruptive aspects of a child's environment. The professional educator wants to know the source of any handicapping condition and provide for remediation if he or she can.

Behavioral Signs of Maltreatment

The professional educator needs to be sensitive to those behavioral signs that experts assert are associated with abuse, even though these signs may sometimes be the result of other traumatic conditions. If the following

signs, when exhibited, are referred to child protective
agency personnel, they provide for the first step in determining whether child abuse and neglect has occurred.
Then, whatever the cause is determined to be, remediation
can be rationally attempted. These behavioral signs include:

- being unduly hostile to authority;
- being excessively distuptive or overly
  aggressive;
- being violent toward classmates;
- contempuously refusing to do or complete
  schoolwork;
- destroying school property and stealing personal
  belongings;
- being extremely passive or withdrawn;
- being a social isolate in both classrooms and on
  the playground;
- being a shy child who is passive and withdrawn and
  who frequently daydreams or cries a lot with
  little apparent reason;
- being a fearful child who is often uncomfortable
  and sometimes threatened in the presence of
  adults and/or seems unduly afraid of parents;
- being unable to attend to lessons for any reasonable length of time;
- being consistently tired and unable to stay awake
  in class;

- being bored during very stimulating activities which appeal to and capture the interest of classmates;
- chronically staying home to take care of other children or parents;
- being frequently absent or truant from school without apparent illness;
- being habitually late for school and/or consistently going home early complaining of illness or related symptoms;
- being consistently absent or indicating abrupt illness on days when scheduled for physical education;
- complaining that physical activity causes pain or discomfort;
- loitering outside the building even after all the staff has gone for the day;
- having a child confide that he or she is having sexual experiences;
- having other children indicate or suggest that the child is being sexually molested or is sexually active.

Once again we wish to stress that the above behaviors characterize many students who are experiencing problems yet are not abused or neglected. It is important that you be tentative in your conclusions and open to new information as you consider the total context within which each observed behavior occurs.

Consider, for example, the so-called "acting out" behaviors. "Acting out" behaviors may be the child's way of asking for help, or they may reflect what the child has learned at home. Perhaps modeling one or both parents, the child lives what he or she has experienced. If the child has experienced violence at home, he or she may tend toward the use of violent behavior at school.

When confronted by an aggressive, belligerent child, educators may find it difficult—some may find it impossible—not to strike back at the child, either physically or verbally. To do so may be a typical response, usually brought on by frustration and sometimes panic. Yet, if educators are to help abused or neglected children shed these old, unacceptable behaviors for new ones, they must adopt positive responses. Seeing the child as a "victim" rather than as an "incorrigible" is a reasonable first step.

However, educators must avoid falling into the trap of feeling so sorry for a supposedly abused or neglected child that they adopt a "laissez-faire, hands-off" approach. They should individualize the child's program, carefully adapting it to his or her needs. They should not treat the child so differently from classmates that the classmates become resentful or the child senses being different. Establishing different norms, reducing expectations, or becoming overly indulgent and permissive may very well aggravate an abused or neglected child's problem.

Educators are often so busy trying to cope with aggressive or uncooperative children that they ignore those who are quiet and withdrawn. Indeed, it is not uncommon to find teachers identifying such children as "model" students. Unfortunately, however, a child who exhibits withdrawing behaviors might be in serious psychological trouble. Educators should be as concerned about this type of child as they are about the physically aggressive or unruly child. Teachers may want to confer with the school psychologist, social worker or counselor when a student appears to be withdrawn, isolated and unable to establish personal relationships with classmates.

When a student is consistently observed "hanging around" before and after classes, school staff may well suspect that something is wrong at home. These behaviors may reflect a home situation characterized by a lack of parental supervision, indifference and perhaps even abuse. In cases where students consistently hang around school, the school staff should plan conferences with the parents to discuss their child's actions. If the situation suggests abuse or possible neglect, a referral should be made.

Physical Signs of Maltreatment

Not only should educators be on the look out for behavioral indicators of possible maltreatment, they should also learn to recognize the physical signs associated with such maltreatment. School staff can learn a great deal about a student's home situation by becoming sensitive to his or her physical appearance. School staff should be especially alert when they observe:

- a child appearing regularly at school wearing inappropriate dress for the weather conditions;
- a child's clothing being far too small or too large to be protective against the elements;
- a child who always wears long sleeve shirts regardless of how warm it is inside or outside the building;
- bruises on the arms or legs, or black eyes;
- burns on the arms or back;
- pulled out hair;
- welts;
- untreated sores;
- a broken arm or jaw;
- a chronically dirty and unkempt child who seldom washes or takes a bath;
- a child who appears infected by parasites or fungus, such as head lice or ring-worm and is not being treated;
- a child who always seems hungry or eats only junk food;
- a child who constantly asks for seconds and thirds during lunch period;

- a child who eats food that is left from classmates' trays;
- a child who steals lunches from other students;
- a child who is unable to refrain from eating during class periods;
- a child who usually brings for lunch only candy, potato chips and other sweets and soda;
- a child who seems to have dental or medical problems which are untreated;
- a child who is lacking in proper immunization;
- a child who shows evidence of dehydration and/or malnutrition;
- a child whose teeth are seriously covered by plaque and he or she has a mouth full of cavities;
- a child who exhibits serious height and weight abnormalities;
- a child who needs a hearing aide or consistently comes to school without it;
- a child who needs glasses and no effort is being made to provide them or repair them if broken;
- a child who has cuts, burns, bruises, etc. and is untreated or inappropriately treated in terms of bandages and medications;
- a child who fails to thrive for no apparent reason.

Obviously, many of these physical signs may be the result of factors other than parental maltreatment. It is not the educator's duty to verify the causes of such conditions, but rather to respond to them if they are manifest.

Instances of any physical trauma should be immediately reported to the school nurse or other appropriately designated official. School staff, except for nurses, should never treat injuries or take the child to a physician without proper (which usually means parental) consent or authority.

Although child neglect can be as serious, or more serious, than some physical injuries caused by abusive treatment, neglect often goes undetected and/or unreported. Educators are sometimes very uncomfortable when they see what may be material neglect but which they think is related to an impoverished home environment. Being aware of the difficulties associated with raising a family under circumstances of poverty or strife, they may believe that calling attention to possible neglect or lack of resources is both unfair and cruel. Not to do so, however, is potentially far more damaging. Thus, one of the prime reasons for reporting these conditions—whatever the cause—is to place these parents in touch with resources that can be helpful to them and to their children.

Continue to Keep Records

Very often there are marginal cases which may not arouse the educator's immediate suspicion. Sometimes it takes a period of weeks or months before a teacher or staff member has reasonable cause to suspect maltreatment. It is helpful, therefore, to continue to keep a dated record book with which to record observations made both before and after reporting.

If a staff member should report a borderline case which later proves to be invalid, he or she should not feel guilty. A report merely suggests the possibility of abuse, neglect, or some other undesirable condition that may require attention and does not automatically stigmatize the family.

WHEN OBSERVING PARENTS

We should be very tentative in our judgements about child abuse until verified information on the parents is available. Indeed, we should suspend judgement altogether until we are informed by trained experts who have studied the parents as well as the referred child. These experts will, of course—in addition to visiting the home, involving health experts, and talking to others—look to us for our observations of both the parents and their children.

It is for this reason that we include the following additional lists of conditions to use as guidelines when observing parents. Fontana (1973) suggests that the presence of child abuse or neglect should be considered a possibility when we observe that parents:

- ignore their child's crying or react with extreme impatience;
- indicate that their child is very "bad" and different from others;
- appear to be of borderline intelligence;
- seem generally irrational;
- appear cruel, sadistic and/or lacking in remorse for hurtful actions.

Helfer (1973) suggests that the presence of abuse should be considered when we observe or learn of parents who:

- show evidence of loss of control, or fear of losing control;
- present contradictory history;
- attribute the cause of injury to a sibling or third party;
- have delayed unduly in bringing the child in for care;
- show detachment;
- reveal inappropriate awareness of seriousness of situation (either overreaction or underreaction);
- continue to complain about irrelevant problems unrelated to the injury;
- personally are misusing drugs or alcohol;
- are disliked, for unknown reasons, by the physician;
- present a history that cannot or does not explain the injury;
- give specific 'eye witness' history of abuse;

- give a history of repeated injury;
- indicate that he or she has no one to 'bail' him or her out when 'up tight' with the child;
- are reluctant to give information;
- refuse consent for further diagnostic studies;
- hospital 'shop';
- cannot be located;
- have been reared in a 'motherless' atmosphere;
- have unrealistic expectations for their child.

Once again, caution should be taken to avoid automatically equating observance of the above conditions with abuse or neglect. While these conditions are often associated with abusive parenting, many who are not abusive also exhibit these same signs. Nevertheless, when one notes these signs the hypothesis of abuse or neglect should be carefully considered and reported for final verification or rejection by child protection staff. Child protective personnel emphasize that they are looking for *patterns,* not isolated behaviors, when they attempt to identify and confirm abuse or neglect.

INCEST: THE CLUES ARE DIFFERENT

Unlike the effects of physical abuse and neglect, there are few obvious physical signs associated with a sexually maltreated child. Furthermore, sexually abused children are often protective of their family and typically are not forthcoming about their experiences. If the child does reveal incestuous experiences, it is usually during a time when a new family crisis is emerging. For example, Goodwin (1982: 5) states that an adolescent may be induced to divulge incest if there is "excessive interference of the father with the child's dating, the initiation of a younger child into the incest, or a rebellious conflict between the child and her father."

Even when a child does reveal sexual maltreatment, there is a tendency among adults to disregard the account. Freud argued that children are prone to incestuous fantasies. Hence a child's revelation of sexual involvement with a parent may be interpreted as an expression of the imagination rather than an actual experience. The unfortunate tendency to not take the child's story seriously is compounded by the fact that children often retract their account upon further questioning by adults.

For example, a child may reveal an incestuous relationship to a teacher who in turn initiates an investigation by professionals. In the interim between the report and the investigation, the parent(s) has ample time to construct a story and to pressure the child into denial. In essence, the child now bears the dual responsibility of having gone public and possibly jeopardizing the family, and further having to deal with the fact that adults outside the family believe he or she has a penchant for "telling stories." Goodwin (1982: 6) claims that less than 4% of child initiated reports of sexual abuse are false. She states:

More common than the incest hoax perpetuated by a child are false retractions of valid incest by a child who is terrified by the impact of her action on her family. These false retractions have, in the past, been counted as incest hoaxes and form much of the (false) experiential basis for believing that children invent incest stories.

Regardless of whether or not the child reveals abuse, there are a number of cues that an astute observer can look for to be alert to the possibility of sexual maltreatment. To some extent, these physical and behavioral symptoms will vary with the age of the victim. While no single characteristic is sufficient evidence of sexual abuse, a consistent pattern should raise the spectre of possible maltreatment. The following are frequently cited characteristics among sexually abused children:

- Frequent bacterial infection, genital rash, and/or chronic vaginal discharge
- Vaginal or rectal bleeding
- Phobias, hysterical seizures, psychosomatic illness, suicide attempts
- Emotional and behavioral problems such as running away, truancy, substance abuse, fear of adults or parents, deep-seated guilt and anxiety, being withdrawn, fits of crying
- Inability to establish positive peer relationships
- Confiding in others about sexual experiences

- Blurting out sexually oriented remarks that seem inappropriate or unlikely considering the person's age or the circumstances
- Drawings or gestures in the context of play-acting that are suggestive of sexual experiences
- In adolescents, sexual promiscuity and prostitution

In addition, teachers, school nurses, counselors and others can pay special attention to children and families who are high risk. For example, children who are handicapped or retarded represent one such high risk group. Also, in families where there is a previous history of abuse, the younger children may become eventual targets. Similarly, in families where there is known to be alcohol abuse, the risk of physical and sexual abuse is greater. Also, in families where the father is somewhat nomadic and away for extended periods of time (e.g., military), or where there is frequent shifting of stepparents and foster children, abuse seems to be greater (Finklehor, 1979). Isolation of the family and overcrowding in the home are also potential risk factors. Finally, families where the father or stepfather and adolescent daughter are in close proximity and the mother is absent or ill, are also at risk. In such cases, the father may jealously guard the daughter from social contact with others, particularly male friends.

In the case of adolescent females, an incestuous relationship may come to light if she becomes pregnant. Although statistics vary, approximately 7 to 10 percent of female adolescent incest victims become pregnant. Not only does this increase the risk of genetic problems, but the psychological risks to the victim are greatly heightened by consanguineous pregnancy. Regardless of whether the cue is pregnancy or some other pattern symptomatic of incest, the responsibility of the observer is to set in motion a process of intervention on behalf of the victim.

SUGGESTED READINGS

Brody, H. and Gaiss, B., "Ethical Issues in Screening for Unusual Child-Rearing Practices." PEDIATRIC ANNALS, Vol. 5, No. 3, March, 1976.

Child Sexual Abuse: Incest, Assault, and Sexual Exploitation, DHHS Pub. No. 81-30166, Revised 1981.

Cohen, S. J., A NATIONAL SURVEY OF ATTITUDES OF SELECTED PROFESSIONALS INVOLVED IN THE REPORTING OF CHILD ABUSE AND NEGLECT. New York: Juvenile Standards Project, Institute of Judicial Administration, Inc., 1974.

Goodwin, Jean, SEXUAL ABUSE: INCEST VICTIMS AND THEIR FAMILIES. Boston: John Wright • PSG Inc., 1982.

Helfer, R. E., "Early Identification and Prevention of Unusual Child-Rearing Practices." PEDIATRIC ANNALS, Vol. 5, No. 3, March, 1976.

Polansky, Norman A., EARLY WARNING SIGNALS OF CHILD ABUSE. Social and Rehabilitation Service Conference on Early Warning Signals of Child Abuse, Atlanta, Georgia, November 27-29, 1973.

Thorman, George, INCESTUOUS FAMILIES. Springfield, IL: Charles C. Thomas, 1983.

7

The Referral Process

Effective reporting procedures will depend to a considerable extent on the leadership provided in each building by administrators, individual staff members and building child abuse and neglect teams (CAN Teams). For the most part, the success of treatment and follow-up care will be contingent upon the quality of school-community relationships established during the referral phase. In this chapter, we examine the various dimensions of the referral process and suggest ways of ensuring an effective response to suspected cases of child maltreatment.

THE ADMINISTRATION OF REPORTING*

The principal is undoubtedly a critical link in the chain of professionals who deal with and respond to the needs of maltreated children. As the school's educational leader, he or she can be expected to assume overall responsibility for managing the school's child abuse and neglect policy.

---

*See *Appendix E* for an illustration of a flow chart for the referral process.

If for some reason this is not possible, the principal should assign this task to a competent professional respected by building staff. The person with the prime responsibility for leadership can be expected to:

- have some knowledge of the nature and scope of reporting procedures and consequences at the national, state and local levels;
- have a working knowledge of reporting procedures required under the state's child abuse and neglect statutes and regulations and their implications for school staff;
- have a working knowledge of the school district's written statement of policy and procedures for reporting;
- have the skills to manage the school's policy and set of procedures for reporting cases of abuse and neglect and have the ability to create and maintain a climate of support and trust which will enable teachers and other staff members to act in a positive, constructive manner when faced by the uncertainties surrounding child abuse and neglect.

Of course, effective leadership will involve eliciting the cooperation of those needed to execute policies. In this regard, the principal will find that a building task force committee will be very helpful in accomplishing effective reporting procedures.

Leadership Initiatives

Informing the Staff of State Laws and Regulations - The principal or the person designated to oversee the reporting process should bring the staff together at the earliest possible date for the express purpose of acquainting them with their state child abuse and neglect statutes and policies. The following items should be explained and clarified regarding language and intent:

- what constitutes child abuse and neglect;
- who is required to report under the law;
- what types of maltreatment must be reported;
- under what conditions must mandated reporters report;
- what are the legal and professional consequences for failing to report;
- what, if anything, are professional educators required to do beyond reporting;
- what protection is built into the law and the reporting process for school staff;
- which state agency is assigned responsibility for investigating and handling child abuse and neglect cases; and
- what are the procedures for follow-up.

The School District's Policy for Reporting - Once the staff has been exposed to the state's child abuse and neglect statute, the next step is to inform them about their school district's policy and the established procedures for dealing with such cases. Specifically, they need such information as:

- the circumstances under which they are obligated and expected to report;
- the steps, if any, they should take prior to reporting;
- the person or persons to whom they should report;
- the school's plan of action upon receiving the teacher's report; and
- the school's assigned role once the department of social services or its equivalent has entered the case, including the specific responsibilities of the school personnel during and after the disposition of the case.

Contact With Community Agencies

Educators form their opinions of child protection agencies and their staffs from what they read, hear and experience. If they rely on second and third party sources, it is possible that they will develop false impressions and negative attitudes toward reporting children to these agencies.

This can be prevented, or at least lessened, by inviting child protective agency case workers to the school to meet and work with the school staff. Face to face contact and the exchange of information and ideas as we suggested in *Chapter 4*, can go a long way in promoting cooperation and mutual respect.

School personnel can benefit from this interaction by learning firsthand from an experienced case worker:

- the department's goals and expectations for identifying and reporting abuse and/or neglect cases;
- the criteria used by the department to determine if actual abuse and/or neglect exists;
- the needs of the department for further information or support once a case has been confirmed;
- the relationship of one agency to another in regard to reporting;
- the typical problems faced by the department when dealing with various types of reported cases; and
- the department's advice and suggestions to school personnel when confronted by possible problems experienced when reporting.

CONFIDENTIALITY OF SCHOOL RECORDS*

When meeting with staff, a block of time should be set aside for the specific purpose of clarifying the relationship of the *Federal Family Rights and Privacy Act*

---

*This section is adapted from *Child Abuse and Neglect Reports*. National Center on Child Abuse and Neglect, DHEW [Publication No. (OHDS) 77-30086], 1977.

(PL 93-380 and its amended form, PL 93-568) to their particular state's child abuse and neglect reporting law. This significant piece of federal legislation is designed to protect parents and their children from unnecessary and potentially damaging public exposure by establishing guidelines governing the release of information from school records.

The fundamental rule for school personnel to follow is that if a school record is to be shared outside the school, the consent of parents is usually required. There are, however, several clear exceptions cited in the regulations that make it possible for the school to bypass the requirement of seeking parental consent prior to disclosing information from school records. For example, the "health or safety emergency" states that:

> An educational agency or institution may disclose personally identifiable information from the education records of a student to appropriate parties in connection with an emergency if knowledge of the information is necessary to protect the health and safety of the student or other individuals.*

Ibid.

To determine if a health and safety emergency condition exists, several factors should be considered. They are:

- the seriousness of the threat to the immediate health or safety of the student or other individual;
- the need for information to meet the emergency;
- whether the parties to whom the information is to be disclosed are in a position to appropriately deal with the emergency; and
- the extent to which time is of the essence in dealing with the emergency.

In actuality, the *Federal Family Educational Rights and Privacy Act* is infrequently an issue since school staff and officials generally learn about cases of abuse and neglect from either personal knowledge or direct observation. In those rare instances when a staff person or official finds something in the child's records which suggests possible abuse or neglect, applying the above standards is an important step before taking the liberty to disclose the information to an appropriate party, which in most cases would be the local child protective agency.

STAFF RESPONSIBILITIES FOR REPORTING

When it comes to identifying and reporting abuse and neglect the school nurse, by virtue of special training and experience, is an especially important member of the school team. The nurse expands and enhances the team's competence by enabling its members to examine the problem from the perspectives of health and medicine. And the nurse functions as the team's health appraiser, health educator and health counselor in cases where known or suspected maltreatment jeopardizes or inhibits the child's ability to perform in school.

As a health appraiser, the school nurse makes observations and gathers information required in assessing the students' health status. It is in this capacity that he or she contributes to the identification of possible victims of abuse and/or neglect. Generally, it is through screening programs and teacher referrals that the problem is brought to the nurse's attention.

Medical and dental screening of kindergarten and elementary school children by professionals is a valuable tool in detecting maltreatment. It enables the school to participate in early diagnostic and preventive measures which serve to protect or save the child from further physical injury or neglect. If through the screening process, signs of child neglect or abuse are observed, the nurse is obligated to report his or her suspicions and take whatever steps are reasonable to help the family meet its parenting responsibilities.

Staff referral is another avenue by which the school nurse is brought into contact with children suffering from some type of maltreatment. The degree to which building staff seek the nurse's help and advice, however, often depends on how effective the nurse has been in establishing rapport and in creating lines of communication. Consequently, if the nurse is to be an effective child advocate in the school setting, time must be devoted to the task of public relations. In the long run, this will be time well spent.

Of course, not all schools employ nurses. Even where they do—for purposes of appropriate identification and reporting of child maltreatment—all school staff share the following responsibilities:

- to become acquainted with their state's child abuse and neglect laws and regulations;
- to develop a working knowledge of their school district's child abuse and neglect policy;
- to be on the alert for signs and symptoms that suggest child abuse and neglect;
- to keep as complete and as specific a set of files recording observations of signs and symptoms as is feasible;
- to report all suspected cases of child abuse and/or neglect to the appropriate school official or state's mandated agency.

Although a school staff member may suspect or know of a case of abuse or neglect, he or she may be somewhat reluctant to report it. Some staff members may:

- operate from the premise that all communication between themselves and their students as clients is confidential and if they learn of the abuse or neglect during a private conference, it is unethical or illegal to divulge it;
- fear that they will alienate the parents if the child's injury turns out to be accidental;
- fear that the student who is moderately or severely abused will be placed in further jeopardy if the parents learn of the referral;
- believe that they alone can handle the situation and affect reasonable change in the behavior of the abusing party without additional professional assistance; or
- believe that the child protective services are not effective in intervening on behalf of the child.

While these concerns are worth examining, they are insufficient when we realize the consequences of not bringing to the children the services and resources of trained professionals.

Some school staff, such as school counselors, social workers and psychologists, may assume that all information they gain during private conferences takes the form of "confidential or privileged communications" and is not to be divulged to any third party. We advise them to examine their state's statutes on this matter to determine exactly their legal obligations under the law. A review of Maine's approach to this question is offered as an illustraiton.

Maine has a "Privileged Communication for School Counselors" statute which states in part that:

> The right of privileged communication shall be extended to school counselors, including but not limited to, elementary and secondary counselors and counselors who may work in a school setting at a post-secondary level.

> A counselor to whom this privilege is granted shall not be required, except as provided in this section, to divulge or to release information which he may have gathered in his counseling relation with said client or, in the case of a minor, the person or agency having legal custody of said minor.

These two paragraphs support the principle of confidentiality and are intended to promote trust and acceptance between counselor and client. However, the last paragraph of the statute establishes a set of conditions which serve to limit the application of this principle in special cases. It reads:

> In the event that the counselee or client's condition is such as to require others to assume responsibility for him, or when there is clear and imminent danger to the counselee or client or to others, the counselor is expected to report this

fact to an appropriate responsible authority or to take such other emergency measures as the situation demands.

In effect, under the Maine Statute, there appear to be three conditions under which a counselor may reveal confidential information (McLaughlin, 1973):

- the client's condition is such as to require others to assume responsibility for him or her;
- when there is clear and imminent danger to the client; or
- when there is clear and imminent danger to others.

In any of these three situations above, the counselor is expected to report the fact to an appropriate responsible authority or take such other emergency measures as the situation demands. In cases where the student informs a school staff member that he or she has been the victim of abuse or neglect, the professional is clearly in a position to reveal this information to a child protective agency. The justification for doing so is found in the conditions listed above as well as in federal and state mandatory child abuse and neglect reporting statutes.

CAN TEAMS

In each building a child abuse and neglect team (CAN Team) should be formed. One example of how a CAN Team might function in the referral process is as follows:

1. Any teacher or other·staff member suspecting child abuse or neglect should immediately convey this information orally to the principal and to the building staff person assigned the responsibility for receiving formal referrals. This person will be the coordinator of the building child abuse/neglect team. Within a period of one working day, a written report should be made on a form provided to the person filing the initial report.

2. A meeting should be promptly called by the principal for the referring staff member and the building child abuse/neglect team (CAN) to discuss alternatives. The purpose of the meeting is to gather and share information relevant to the child and his or her family. At this time, the child protective services agency should be notified to determine if they should become involved.

3. *If* deemed appropriate under the circumstances, the child should be observed in school or interviewed in private by a trained staff member of the same gender as the child. The goal is to obtain as much information from the child as possible without making the child feel uncomfortable. However, this step should not be taken without the consultation or direction of an

authorized person from the appropriate child protective services agency. If the child is willing, the
school nurse might examine him or her *without* re-
moving clothing covering the genital area. If the interview seems to confirm the suspicion of abuse or
neglect, a report should be written immediately and
submitted by the coordinator of the CAN Team.

4. The principal or other designated coordinator of the
CAN team should promptly contact the appropriate
social service or law enforcement agency and request
that an agency representative meet with school staff
and receive a written report. In order to expedite the
reporting process, the standardized reporting form of
the school district should be used in all buildings.
(Examples of such a form can be found in the appendices. A sample of the reporting form should also be
included in the policy statement.)

5. The coordinator of the CAN Team or a school counselor or social worker (or other trained person who is
also a member of the building CAN Team) should be
assigned to follow-up on the agency's progress in dealing with the child and his or her family. Teachers and
other relevant school staff should be given as much
feedback as possible, within the bounds of professional
ethics, as the case develops.

WORDS OF CAUTION

School staff should not assume the role of being investigators unless specifically authorized. School staff, in the initial stages, should limit themselves to identifying and reporting. They should avoid trying to verify on their own that it is or is not an actual case of child abuse or neglect. Verification is not the responsibility of school personnel. The school staff should not take matters into their own hands regardless of how competent they may be. For example, contacting parents independently may only cause problems for the school and more pain to the child.

Unless given the proper authority, never take physically abused children to a physician or hospital for treatment. The appropriate authorities should be informed so they can take whatever action is necessary. Parental consent is generally required in such instances, and the state's child abuse and neglect law details the limits of protection afforded professionals.

In summary, school staff members should not put off reporting a suspected case of abuse or neglect nor should they assume that the situation will not repeat itself. Chances are that if the child has been abused once, he or she will be abused again. If it is a first time, a report could very well save the child from further abuse.

SUGGESTED READINGS

Education Commission of the States, CHILD ABUSE AND NEGLECT IN THE STATES: A DIGEST OF CRITICAL ELEMENTS OF REPORTING AND CENTRAL REGISTRIES. Child Abuse and Neglect Project, Denver, Colorado, Report No. 83, March, 1976.

McKenty, S. B., CHILD ABUSE: A MULTIDISCIPLINARY INTERAGENCY PROGRAM FOR IDENTIFICATION AND REFERRAL. FINAL PROGRAM STATUS REPORT. Office of Education (DHEW), Washington, D. C., June 30, 1976. (This monograph illustrates the implementation of a child abuse program in Texas.)

Wald, M., "The Role of Schools in Child Protective Services." GUIDELINES FOR PUPIL SERVICES, Vol. 10, No. 3, May, 1972.

8

Relating to Families

The commitment of schools to resolving the problem of child abuse and neglect should not rest once policies have been formulated and a program implemented for identifying and reporting children who suffer from" maltreatment. School employees will need to know how to effectively relate to abused or neglected students and their parents after identification and reporting have occurred. What are the unique problems faced by teachers, school counselors, school social workers, principals, and other staff as they relate to children who have been identified as maltreated or formerly maltreated? How should school personnel respond to the parents of these children? The purpose of this chapter is to suggest practical guidelines for school staff.

SCHOOL STAFF GUIDELINES

As we indicated before, caution should be taken when attempting to construct a social profile of abusive parents. The general social and' psychological patterns which may characterize a number of parents may or may not be applicable when trying to understand specific cases of child abuse. The various dimensions of child abuse do not readily fit into standard psychiatric categories. Each family situation is unique and therefore requires careful investigation in its own right. Likewise, each family will require individualized therapeutic programs geared to meet its specific needs. Nevertheless, there are a number of guidelines that can help direct school staff when relating to abusive parents and maltreated children.

Use A Team Approach

Perhaps we need to emphasize again that the school is not solely responsible for working out the problems of abusive families. There are instances in the past where schools have attempted to do all the investigative and therapeutic work with these children and their parents to the exclusion of social service agencies. Such a complex task is beyond the school's sphere of competence and legal authority. Indeed, solitary efforts by the school to solve the problem may make matters worse. Schools need the assistance of other professionals and should attempt to develop ameliorative strategies in conjunction with these professionals. Lack of coordination between service agencies and the schools should be avoided. A *team approach* to the problem has the greatest chance of being successful.

The Responsibility for Coordination

At least one professional staff member in each school—perhaps a school social worker, nurse, psychologist or counselor—should be charged with the responsibility of maintaining contact with the various agencies (police, social workers, protective service units, hospitals, etc.) who become involved. Of course, care should be taken when working with professionals in other agencies that criticism of their performance not be communicated. Perceptions of implied criticism are likely to hinder cooperation. It should be obvious that the staff person contacting these agencies should attempt to elicit as much support and as many practical suggestions as possible. If at all appropriate, the impression should be conveyed that the school is grateful for assistance and that feedback is in the best interest of the students involved.

Work With Service Agencies

Casework information from service agencies is especially important to classroom teachers, nurses, school counselors, social workers and psychologists. Oftentimes, maltreated children experience learning difficulties stemming directly from their family situation. Abusive parents, through their use of strict controls and harsh punishments, may inadvertently inhibit their child's development in school. This can result in learning barriers such as listlessness in the classroom, poor attention span, inability to retain information, inability to work autonomously, or any number of other problems.

In order to overcome such learning problems, educators need to devise individual education plans of study tailored to the special educational needs of each maltreated child. It is fortunate that educators are increasingly accepting the regulations of *Public Law* 94-142. Of course, an individualized program has the greatest chance of being successful if the classroom teacher can organize and implement it in light of detailed information concerning the unique conditions of the student's family. It is imperative that the school employee responsible for compiling casework information keep teachers and other school staff informed. Likewise, school staff should not hesitate to make frequent inquiries to the person doing follow-up work on each case. Continual contact with the case is the best way to foster understanding of each child's special needs.

Involve the Other School Staff

Just as teachers can play a major role in providing support and assistance to children, so too can school counselors, social workers and psychologists make their contribution to the emotional well-being of students and parents.

The primary responsibilities of these professionals reside in the areas of investigative assistance, coordination of service and therapy under the guidance of child protective agency staff.

Although child protective agencies are responsible for doing case investigations after a referral has been made, professional school social workers, counselors and psychologists can certainly offer to assist in this process. Very often child protective agencies are working with rather limited resources and simply may not be able to conduct as much background research on each case as would be desirable. Hence, useful information might be lost. For example, school social workers could assist by talking with such people as cafeteria workers who see what the child eats, or with bus drivers who will see the child in another setting. They may also assist in constructing case histories of the child by using available school records and interviews with teachers.

Remember, one of the most important contributions that any school staff member can make is to volunteer his or her services to those legally mandated to intervene for the child's welfare. Many times school nurses, psychologists, social workers and counselors can be uniquely employed by child protective services staff in ways they may not have anticipated but which prove to be invaluable to the children.

Perhaps the most important role to be played by these professionals, when requested, is in the area of follow-up.* The school is obligated to follow-up the investigations and treatment of child protective services as well as the child's progress in school if the child's educational development is jeopardized. Only with complete follow-up is it possible to design effective individualized educational plans. By serving as an official link between the child protective team and the rest of the school staff, and through their knowledge of available state and community resources, these professionals can be valuable resource persons for parents and educators alike.

Respect Confidentiality

Although it may seem obvious, it is important to remind all school staff about the rights of parents and children to confidentiality. Instances of child abuse and neglect may seem like interesting topics for coffee room discussions or out of school conversations. However, divulging information about a student's family life should be done only under ethically proper circumstances. A student's classmates, neighbors, school volunteers, etc.

---

*See *Appendix F* for a sample continuous follow-up form for use by school staff.

should not have access to such privy information. Rumors which impune the reputation of a family (even if the rumors are true) may function to further isolate that family from needed help and retard the success of therapeutic efforts.

RELATING TO THE CHILD

Educators should consider how the abused or neglected child might construct a view of the world. Feelings of fear, rejection, emotional separation from the family and a pervasive sense of powerlessness are typical among maltreated children. These children may attempt to isolate themselves from family members and from others as a way of coping with their insecurities and avoiding conflict. They may have learned that it's best not to trust others and hence they may not seek assistance for themselves. If this pattern continues, these children may have difficulty in establishing necessary intimate bonds with family members, with peers and with other adults as well. Unless educators are perceptive of these avoidance patterns, the maltreated child may not secure aid in dealing with such emotional difficulties.

Develop Trusting Relationships

Very often classroom teachers, with a little effort, can develop trusting relationships with their students. Not only can teachers serve as adult role models, but they can also function in a therapeutic capacity by being approachable, patient listeners. Teachers and other school staff should do all they can to provide the kind of support system where children feel that they can discuss their problems. Initially, abused children may feel shame, embarrassment, or guilt about their family life and be reluctant to express any of their feelings openly. Perhaps the child has even been ordered by the parents to remain silent. Thus, educators should not pressure the child to self-disclose. Rather, by showing empathy and a patient willingness to listen without being critical or negative toward the child or the child's parents, the child may eventually express pent-up feelings. Such self-disclosure is often an important first step in coming to terms with deep-seated fears and a poor self image. Finally, pay special attention to conversational topics which the child repeats or dwells upon; these suggest concerns of greatest relevance to the child.

Foster Relationships With Peers

One thing educators can do to assist abused or neglected children is to help them establish positive relationships with their peers at school. Positive peer relationships are especially crucial for maltreated children. Maltreated children may not be able to develop healthy relationships with adults. For them, the nature of their relationships with their peers is extremely important. School-related extra-curricular activities represent one area in which educators can encourage involvement. Team sports, clubs, volunteer groups, Boy Scouts and Girl Scouts, etc., are just a few activities that can increase an abused child's interaction with peers as well as with adults. While trying to extend a child's network of close peer affiliation may not alter parental patterns of maltreatment, it does help to reduce his or her isolation and enhance the possibility of establishing meaningful personal relations with others.

Be Careful In Questioning

All school staff should keep in mind certain rules of thumb when questioning students who are maltreated. While it is the duty of all school staff to initiate the reporting process when a student's appearance or behavior is suspicious, the staff should avoid repeated questioning of the student. Such probing can be traumatic for the student and can usually best be conducted within the professional bounds of case work. It is not the teacher's responsibility to determine whether the abuse was intentional or what conditions were surrounding the incident. Likewise, other school staff should not call or visit the child's parents or relatives when questions of abuse or neglect arise unless under the specific direction of protective agency staff. Regardless of how upsetting the situation may be, remember to approach the child with a sense of warmth and understanding without communicating to him or her that you are passing judgements.

Individualize Instruction But Be Careful

Once teachers and other school staff have the necessary information to develop an individualized program, they should be particularly mindful of the manner in which this program is presented to the child. Educators should be careful not to let the child realize that he or she is being singled out for special treatment. Any special assistance should appear to the child as a natural part of his or her curriculum. It should also appear that way to other children.

It is of crucial importance when one is working with a maltreated child that one should avoid conveying the impression that the child's parents are inadequate or unloving. Never be openly critical of the parents in front of the child or other students! In this regard, educators should make a conscious effort to avoid conferring upon the child or his parents a "deviant" label. The school staff should be pleasant and provide as supportive an environment at school as possible and leave treatment of the home situation to child protective services.

In conjunction with the above, teachers and other school staff should take care not to be critical of the child to parents in cases of poor academic performance. It is important to give the child additional attention and positive reinforcement whenever possible. Criticism from the school can add unnecessary pressure to the child's home situation and may even be an excuse for further maltreatment. Discretionary corporal punishment should not be employed in cases where the child is subject to physical abuse at home. If anything, the maltreated child should perceive all school staff as warm and caring persons—as "special friends" with whom he or she can confide.

Teachers and other school staff, however, should not focus attention on the maltreated child in such a way as to make other children feel ignored or offended. All too often in human relationships, we unwittingly hurt or anger one person by trying to reassure and help another. The goal is to establish supportive adult relationships without creating estrangements from peers. Such efforts make sense in any relationship but are especially important when dealing with abused and neglected children.

Do Not Display Pity

Although maltreated children usually do not seek or want pity, some will welcome the opportunity to discuss their family situation with a staff member that they regard as a special friend. Although the teacher is certainly not expected to resolve all of the conflicts a maltreated child may experience, just giving this child the opportunity to vent frustrations can be therapeutic. The teacher or other staff members can help the child to articulate feelings and realize that his or her inhibitions are normal. Getting children to talk about their feelings can be both personally satisfying and a source of self-realization. However, at the first sign that a child may be abused or neglected, protective service personnel should be involved for their guidance.

Be Consistent and Develop Trust

Educators should also be aware that one of the problems maltreated children must cope with is parental inconsistency in child-rearing behavior. This inconsistency can be the source of a general mistrust of all forms of adult authority. Children need supportive and consistent adult role models to serve as positive reference persons that can be trusted. Thus, it is especially important that teachers act in a consistent fashion, providing guidance and conveying clear-cut expectations to children.

WHEN RELATING TO PARENTS

It is very important to find out if parental maltreatment is situational or chronic. The child protective agency staff will be in the best position to come to a conclusion about this and may give the information to you. Situational abuse or neglect may be a one-time occurrence due to a particularly stressful situation (e.g., loss of job, parent in hospital, death in family, etc.). In these cases, the damage to the child is usually not severe or enduring and the parents are typically remorseful and willing to accept help. Chronic abuse or neglect, on the other hand, is far more serious. It reflects a patterned set of behaviors which may be well established as part of parent-child interactions.

Thus, child protective services personnel working directly with parents must conduct an intense analysis of parental techniques of child management in order to establish the reasons for abuse or neglect rather than to punish the parents. That is, it is geared toward eliminating the motivating factors associated with abuse. Actual treatment goals, therefore, will vary with each family situation.

Maintain Emotional Self-Control

The initial step all school staff must take is to come to terms with their own feelings about the problem. The proper professional stance with respect to maltreated children and their parents should be one of objectivity. School staff should never convey a sense of admonition or moral revulsion to the parents. If anything, they should attempt to convey a feeling of understanding and support. Abusive parents need reassurance and the opportunity to feel good about themselves if they are to stop being abusive. This is especially important if the parents are already feeling isolated or hostile.

Avoid Issuing Warnings

Teachers and other school staff may sometimes feel that they can prevent further abuse by warning a family that a report will be made if the abuse or neglect continues. Such action is seldom effective and may even put the child at greater risk. Protective agency staff are usually trained in interviewing techniques and case investigation and are professionally equipped to move closer to the situation. In this regard, the educator's primary responsibility is to call attention to suspected cases and to maintain contact with those doing the actual casework.

Do Not Become An Adversary

One problem that child protective service workers encounter is parent reluctance to admit that the child has been abused, accompanied by parent denial of culpability. Such denials may be based on fear of social retribution or may simply be a defense against guilt. Because of their defensiveness, parents who are maltreating their children may be rather hostile and defensive during encounters with school staff. School staff should be on guard not to be placed in the role of adversary.

It is important to have good rapport with parents while working with them, and when working with them, they may admit to a problem. This is usually a good sign which, along with the details of all your relations with parents, should be communicated to the child protective agency in charge. Again, we repeat, no relationships between school staff and parents of maltreated children should ever occur without the awareness and support of the child protective agency staff who are legally mandated to work with abusive or neglecting parents.

When school staff work with abusive parents, it is not their responsibility to correct the abusive behavior. In communications with abusive parents at school, school staff should keep their discussions limited to questions of school activity unless specifically directed otherwise by protective service workers. And remember, never communicate to parents the feeling that you are passing judgement on them regardless of how they treat their children.*

WHAT TO EXPECT

Many educators realize that neither their professional training nor their personal experiences adequately prepare them for encounters with abused children. Given the importance of effective communication with these children, it may be helpful to keep the following points in mind:

---

*See *Appendix F* for an illustration of a hypothetical school response to a hypothetical case of neglect.

- Don't expect any "miracle cures." Victims of abuse often have experienced a pattern of maltreatment extending over months or years. As such, the child may have developed various strategies to help him or her cope but which are troubling to you (e.g., withdrawal). Therefore don't be discouraged if your efforts do not meet with immediate success.

- Don't expect abused children to automatically feel a debt of gratitude to you. Many abused children have learned not to trust adults and are unable to express thanks when help is offered. However a child's failure to express his or her sentiments does not mean that your efforts are unsuccessful.

- Don't expect all abused children to be the same or to have identical needs. No single approach is applicable to all. Similarly, your relationship with the child should develop naturally without seeming contrived or forced. However, being patient, empathetic, and honest with children nearly always is a precondition for successful intervention.

SUGGESTED READINGS

Ebeling, Nancy, and Hill, Deborah, CHILD ABUSE AND NEGLECT: A GUIDE WITH CASE STUDIES FOR TREATING THE CHILD AND THE FAMILY. Boston: John Wrights • PSG, Inc., 1983.

Fontana, Vincent J., SOMEWHERE A CHILD IS CRYING: MALTREATMENT CAUSES AND PREVENTION. New York: MacMillan, 1973.

Part C
The School and Preventive Services

9
Assisting Parents, Students and Staff: School Health Workers

The primary difference between *protective* and *preventive* services is that protective services are almost exclusively a court and/or state agency responsibility. For children who are abused and neglected, the child protective services agency is charged with the responsibility of their protection. Of course, schools, hospitals and other community groups must be involved in protecting maltreated children. However, it is the child protective service agency in your area which has the authority for investigation, coordination, supervision and delivery of services. Obviously, a child protective service agency represents the community's official responsibility to intervene to safeguard a child's welfare when the parents are unable to do so.

On the other hand, preventive services are designed to help families so that the community does not have to intervene. In this sense, any organization that helps parents develop more healthy relationships with their children can be seen as providing preventive services even if that is not its explicit goal. Clearly, when any organization or individual helps to lessen the problems of parenting, it is

engaged in the prevention of abuse and neglect. Whatever
the school does to help prevent the occurrence of family
disorganization (through community education parenting
programs, in-school parenting education, programs for
enhancing community awareness, professional development activities regarding prevention, working with parents
and children through guidance and counseling programs,
etc.) should be considered "preventive services".

Of course, there is no legal obligation for schools to
involve child protective service agencies in all of their prevention efforts. However, it is increasingly being recognized that while it may not be legally necessary, it makes
good sense to have concerned public and private groups
working together.

Child protective service agencies recognize that prevention is essential and in many communities they are
trying to foster preventive services in both public and
private organizations as well as among community volunteers. They can be of considerable assistance in coordinating and reducing the duplication of efforts. More importantly, child protection service agencies can often help
schools to be more effective in programming through
the use of resources already at their disposal. With these
ideas in mind, we suggest that various components of the
school—classroom teachers, community educators, school
health workers, etc.—work among themselves and with
local child protective agency personnel to examine their
opportunities and resources.

Each component will have its own special opportunities and need for resources. For example, school social workers sometimes work with parents who come to them for assistance with problems which, if unattended, may lead to abuse or neglect.

SCHOOL COUNSELORS, PSYCHOLOGISTS AND SOCIAL WORKERS

It is not difficult to understand why teachers sometimes respond to problem behaviors in school without adequate recognition of the various dimensions of the problem. Too much to do for too many pupils is no doubt a contributing factor. In some schools where "unusual behavior" is viewed as a rule infraction warranting immediate and decisive corporal punishment, some children may suffer further difficulty. However, there are many schools which interpret unusual behavior as a warning sign that the child is in trouble and needs special help. It is the latter interpretation which contributes to best defining the roles of counselors, psychologists and social workers in preventing child abuse and neglect. This is true because such staff professionals are likely to have the specific training, expertise and opportunity needed for working with individuals in emotional and social crises. The professional support staff also occupy roles which allow them to coordinate and mobilize resources for which teachers and others simply do not have the time. And, even if teachers and other school staff "know" what accounts for the problems of their children, there is no guarantee that they will be able to cope with them or remedy the situation.

Helping Teachers and Other Staff

School counselors, social workers and psychologists are in a particularly favorable position to help in the prevention of abuse and neglect by assisting teachers and other staff. They can perform a vital service by:

- helping teachers discover why problem pupils feel and behave as they do;
- helping teachers, when appropriate, handle their feelings toward these children;
- helping teachers, when appropriate, develop specific strategies to meet the needs of these children; and
- helping teachers, where appropriate, carry out these strategies and evaluate their effectiveness.

Since emotionally troubled children often experience learning difficulties in school (Kline, 1977), some teachers may assume that academic remedial procedures alone will produce the desired outcomes of increased academic achievement. However, research studies suggest, as most educators recognize, that emotional and social conditions are important variables affecting school learning. Children with social and emotional problems often have views about themselves which serve as obstacles to school learning and social adjustment. Such self-images can precipitate serious problems at home. It becomes necessary, therefore, for all school staff to promote healthy self-concept development among children.

Working With Students

Social and emotional health specialists in schools can also be a positive force in the lives of children in order to prevent their maltreatment or their later becoming abusive or neglecting parents. In fact, a comprehensive preventive services program will include the provision of professional assistance for children who are not abused or neglected but who have emotional or social problems. Many of these children will experience difficulty in establishing positive relationships with their parents which can lead to crisis periods for them at home or which can hinder their developing into healthy parents themselves one day. Extended patterns of conflict for a child with siblings or peers can be a catalyst for serious conflict with parents. The special educator, school social worker, psychologist or counselor needs to work with such children or be able to refer them to those who can help them with their problems.

However, whatever specific objectives school professionals set for themselves in providing treatment to such students, they should be guided by their legal authority, training and level of expertise. For example, Peters (1968) warns that children with serious problems who need special therapeutic counseling can be harmed if they are treated only by school counselors rather than by specialists equipped to handle the unique demands of these children. The argument that no other specialist is available in many schools, he asserts, does not give license to a school counselor to go beyond his or her competencies.

Many treatment modalities are available with respect to the type of relationship that a counselor, social worker or psychologist might attempt to establish in working directly with students. Given that each situation is unique, it would be presumptuous for us to state the type of modality any professional should employ. The purpose here is to merely focus attention on the fact that when working with students who have social or emotional problems and who are not now the recipients of abuse or neglect, social and emotional health specialists can do much to prevent abuse or neglect in the future for some of these students. While school staff may find that they cannot control what goes on outside of the school, they can help provide support for children in school. They can help to make school more pleasant for socially or emotionally impaired students, and that in itself will make a contribution to the prevention of child maltreatment.

Again, we repeat, when working closely with students with serious problems, school staff have particularly good reason for maintaining contact with child protective agency staff. School staff are in a very good position for identifying students who are "high risk" candidates for abuse or neglect in the future.

Helping Identify Potential Maltreatment

Effective identification of potential for child maltreatment should be an important part of any complete prevention program and school health workers should be involved in this effort. However, there is need for caution. There are many lists of guidelines available for use in identifying potential abuse and neglect. Some of these guidelines may be very helpful but a large number of them seem to us to be of questionable utility unless thoroughly considered. This is another reason for involving child protective service professionals for their input. Protective service personnel will be aware of many alternatives and ideas for helping parents.

If the school health workers are to be effective in assisting in the prevention of child maltreatment, then they must also plan to work with parents. Although classroom teachers can and should meet periodically with all parents, they usually have neither the time nor the training to cope with the special needs and problems of parents who voluntarily come to school staff seeking assistance in working with their children. Of the school's special services personnel, school social workers, counselors and psychologists are probably most suited for this role.

Keeping in mind that the school is not legally responsible for helping parents relate to their children, the school health worker should carefully delineate between his or her role and that of other health workers in the community, e.g., child guidance agency personnel. Doing so may prove somewhat difficult given the inevitable overlap when dealing with people and their problems. However, since school social workers, counselors and psychologists are often links between the school and the parents, we suggest that their goal should be to improve the *child's chances for optimal educational experience.* During this process, they may find it helpful to provide formal therapy or counseling to parents, which in turn may help them deal more adequately with their children, or they may decide to work with the whole family.

Helping Parents Help Their Children

Since child maltreatment is often a problem of improper parenting rather than a psychiatric disorder, part of prevention should consist of educating parents to proper child care and its relationship to physical, social, emotional and educational growth. Many parents are unaware of the normal stages of physical and cognitive growth among children and thus hold unrealistic expectations for their offspring. The child's failure to meet these unrealistic expectations can become a reason for abuse. The school social worker, psychologist and counselor are in strategic positions to provide knowledge about these processes and to offer suggestions and possible demonstrations on how to promote their development.

When meeting with neglectful parents—those who ignore are indifferent to their child's needs—the school social worker can offer various kinds of advice and assistance. Consider, for example, the possible problem of a child's need for structure:

- *The child's need for structure.* Some parents may assume too much of a *laissez-faire,* permissive attitude toward their children. They may fail to establish rules by which to help them structure their daily living.
- Their children may have to depend too much on their own resources, no matter how limited and ill-defined. They may carry a heavy burden since their behavior and style of living may conflict with school-based norms and expectations. A consequence is that they may be more likely to do poorly in school than their classmates.

- Parents may be inconsistent with discipline or send
  contradictory messages to their children concerning appropriate conduct. As a result, it becomes
  difficult for the child to develop socially acceptable
  behavior.

These specialists can help parents understand that
children need direction and clearly defined rules to follow.
They can explain how this knowledge can enhance their
children's feelings of security and personal safety. And
they can assist parents in formulating a framework of
rules for their children to follow.

School professionals who are working with parents
who are not suspected of being abusive to or neglecting
their children may discuss alternative techniques of child
management. If non-abusive parents come to school and
ask for help in handling their children, and school personnel are competent to provide advice, they should do so.
If not, they should immediately refer the parents to community agencies which can be of help. This means that the
school staff should be well aware of all family and children
services available and how to make appropriate referrals.

THE SCHOOL NURSE

In the health education role, the school nurse is able
to meet the needs of individual students by informal teaching of health concepts and practices during conferences
with them and/or their parents. Initiatives of this sort can
be especially valuable in helping overcome problems which
might eventually trigger abuse or neglect. Additionally,
the school nurse is a primary resource person in educating

teachers and school personnel to the various dimensions of child maltreatment and how it emerges, such that school staff may plan for a more healthy environment.

As a health counselor, the school nurse focuses on the tasks required to assist students and their families in achieving greater self-sufficiency in decreasing their health problems. This may take the form of health-care workshops for families or of the school nurse counseling parents as to appropriate medical, dental and social resources available in the community. This implies that the school nurse must have sound working knowledge of the community's health and medical care network (Berg et al., 1973).

This enhanced role of the school nurse is reflected in the position statement prepared jointly by the American Nurses' Association and the American School Health Association and published in *The Journal of School Health*. The chart on the following page lists the kinds of activities these two organizations believe today's well-trained school nurse can perform. It is our view that if the school nurse successfully carries out some of these initiatives, he or she will be a powerful ally in the prevention of child abuse and neglect. We suggest, however, that the list reflects an ideal toward which to work rather than what school personnel can reasonably expect of a single nurse, or even several nurses in a district, to accomplish in a short time. Moreover, we recommend that school nurses work within teams of school and community professionals rather than alone since the problem is of a multidisciplinary nature and cannot be solved by any one agency or professional.

In summary, the school nurse contributes to the prevention of the child abuse and neglect problem by applying health and medical care expertise to the areas of identification, education and counseling. Such knowledge and skill in using the community's health and medical care network is of vital importance to the school's ability to play a constructive role in preventing abuse and neglect.

The Changing Role of the School Nurse

The American Nurses' Association and the American School Health Association have suggested that school nurse practitioners should, within the area of their competence, be able to perform the following activities:

- *Serve as a health advocate for the child;*
- *Assist parents in assuming greater responsibility for health maintenance of the child, and provide relevant health instruction, counseling and guidance;*

- *Contribute to the health education of individuals and groups, and apply methods designed to increase each person's motivation to assume responsibility for his own health care;*
- *Assess and arrange appropriate management and referrals for children with health problems who require further evaluations and care by their personal physicians or others, and collaborate with them in decision-making involving health care and services;*
- *Collaborate with teachers and other school personnel in interpreting pupil health status and provide guidance regarding adjustments and management of educational and health programs for students with special needs;*
- *Identify the health status of the child by securing and evaluating a thorough health and developmental history, and record the findings succinctly and systematically;*
- *Perform a physical examination;*
- *Initiate, perform, and assess appropriate preventive and screening tests, and refer for diagnostic, clinical, and laboratory procedures;*
- *Perform developmental evaluations and screening tests; participate with other health and educational professionals in assessing normal variations and abnormalities of motor, cognitive, and perceptual aspects of child development; and assist in managing health problems;*

- *Assist in determining the presence of significant emotional disturbances and psychoeducational problems in childhood and adolescence, and in planning for the referral and management of these problems;*
- *Provide appropriate emergency health services;*
- *Advise and counsel students concerning acute and chronic health problems, and assume responsibility for appropriate intervention, management and referral;*
- *Make home visits when indicated for effective management of health problems;*
- *Participate in providing anticipatory guidance and counseling to parents concerning problems of child rearing, including those related to developmental crises, common illness, accidents, dental health, and nutrition;*
- *Participate in developing and coordinating health care plans involving family, school, and community to enhance the quality of health care and to diminish both fragmentation and duplication of services;*
- *Assess and evaluate nursing practice in the school setting;*
- *Identify community resources.*

INCEST INTERVENTION

The process of intervening in cases of sexual abuse is essentially the same as that for physical maltreatment and neglect (Mayer 1983). Again we wish to stress that the emotional trauma of the abuse can be increased if the family becomes embroiled in an array of confusing and insensitive bureaucratic routines. Fear of family disintegration and public stigma make this an emotionally charged time for both the child and the parents.

As an educator, you can help in the recovery process in several ways. As previously mentioned, being a sensitive, approachable listener or special friend to the child is important. Never express a sense of disgust or moral aversion toward the child or the parents concerning what has transpired. You can help by attempting to structure age-appropriate activities for the child that will enhance his or her sense of autonomy while simultaneously extending the social network beyond the family. School programming can also include constructive parent-child activities that will help them to rectify the damage to their relationship. Finally, be patient. The disruption following intervention can be overcome by coordination with appropriate agencies and a willingness on your part to respond to the emotional needs of the child. Trust that both the child and his or her family are capable of emerging from this on a much healthier footing.

Regarding programming, school and classroom activities for the primary prevention of sexual abuse require a much more detailed discussion and presentation than is possible here. Fortunately, however, there are many educational materials which include lesson plans and guides which are now available. They allow any teacher or adult working with children or adolescents to provide activities and information that will increase prevention skills and foster healthy attitudes. Participants in such programs will become more resistant to sexual abuse and they will be less likely to become abusive parents themselves. Some of these materials are:

CHILD SEXUAL ABUSE PREVENTION PROJECT: An Educational Program for Children. Cordelia Kent. Sexual Assault Services, Hennepin County Attorney's Office, C-2000 Government Center, Minneapolis, MN 55487, 1979. A guidebook for preventing sexual abuse through education.

PERSONAL SAFETY: Curriculum for Prevention of Child Sexual Abuse. Maryl Olson. Child Sexual Abuse Prevention Program, Skyline Elementary School, 2301 North Mildred, Tacoma, WA 98406. For teachers of grades K-8.

PERSONAL SAFETY CURRICULUM. Geraldine Crisci. (Available in English and Spanish). Child Sexual Abuse Prevention Project, Franklin/Hampshire Community Mental Health Center, 79 Pleasant Street, Northampton, MA 01060. For grades preschool-6.

PREVENTING SEXUAL ABUSE: Activities and Strategies for Those Working with Children and Adolescents. Carol A. Plummer. Learning Publications, Inc., P.O. Box 1326, Holmes Beach, FL 33509.

STRATEGIES FOR FREE CHILDREN: A Leader's Guide to Child Assault Prevention. Child Assault Prevention Project. Women Against Rape, P.O. Box 02084, Columbus, OH 43202.

VICTIMS ALL: A Teaching Guide for Child Abuse and Neglect Prevention. Anthony Citrin. Learning Publications, Inc., P.O. Box 1326, Holmes Beach, FL 33509.

SUGGESTED READINGS

Education Commission of the States, EDUCATION FOR PARENTHOOD, A PRIMARY PREVENTION STRATEGY FOR CHILD ABUSE AND NEGLECT. Denver, Colorado, Report No. 93, December, 1976.

Forrer, S. E., "Battered Children and Counselor Responsibility," SCHOOL COUNSELOR, Vol. 22, No. 3, January, 1975.

Litwack, J. and Litwack, L., "The School Nurse as a Health Counselor." JOURNAL OF SCHOOL HEALTH, December, 1976.

Mayer, Adele, CHILD SEXUAL ABUSE, Holmes Beach, FL: Learning Publications Inc., 1984.

Plummer, Carol, PREVENTING SEXUAL ABUSE, Holmes Beach, FL: Learning Publications, Inc., 1984.

10

Educational Planning for Prevention

Difficult though it may seem, schools can do many things in their regular curriculum with little in the way of added funds to help prevent child abuse from occurring. Some kinds of innovative programs will, of course, require special funding. Even so, some added expenditures may seem far less costly when it is recognized that what schools do to help prevent child abuse in their regular programming contributes to the attainment of their traditional academic and social goals. Successful curriculum planning for the prevention of child abuse and neglect is no less than a basic part of any comprehensive program for all children. And, like any other successful component of schooling, it is usually built with the cooperation of many school and community persons. To be successful, educational programming for the prevention of child maltreatment must be based on the cooperation and shared needs of the entire school staff, agency personnel, parents, students and the community.

In addition to cooperation there is, of course, the need to be informed. A general lack of awareness has probably been a significant factor retarding prevention efforts in the past. In order to establish an effective prevention program, it is essential to have accurate information concerning the nature and extent of the problem in the school's community. In other words, how widespread is child abuse and neglect in the school and community? What are the most pressing needs of those affected? As mentioned in *Chapter 5,* the schools, in conjunction with other community agencies, should contribute to the establishment of a research oriented task force responsible for gaining information on child abuse and neglect. Ultimately, this knowledge will be used to identify the most serious aspects of the problem in the community, establish immediate priorities and set long range goals.

PREVENTION PROGRAMS

School districts already have a wide range of resources and an existing dissemination network which, if harnessed effectively, can serve to help prevent child abuse and neglect. In light of their resources for information dissemination, one of the best ways schools can contribute to the prevention of child maltreatment is by initiating educational programs for different groups in the school and community. Such an educational campaign would require developing special curricula tailored to meet the unique needs of each group. This program would include: 1) general courses which will help prepare all students for parenthood; 2) special services for students who are parents or about to become parents; 3) courses for parents in the community; 4) courses for school and service agency personnel; and 5) a general consciousness raising program for the community at large.

Preparing All Students for Parenthood

While schools have been relatively successful in teaching students basic academic skills, comparatively little has been done to prepare them for parenthood and the problems and responsibilities of family life. Although some progress has been made in recent years, there is still an overwhelming need for curriculum development in sex education, human development and family living. Such an emphasis in school could well have a major impact in reducing the likelihood that future parents will mistreat their offspring. These courses could be readily incorporated into the regular curriculum, especially at the junior high and high school levels.

A basic "parenthood education" program should include a number of specific content areas. To begin, we believe it is of fundamental importance that schools provide comprehensive sex education to all students. Included here would be an understanding of human sexual functioning, personal hygiene, reproduction, knowledge of birth control options, as well as the responsibilities associated with emotional commitments. All too often ignorance of one's own body results in unanticipated and unwanted children, who in turn are subjected to abuse or neglect. Sex education is especially important when one considers the fact that there are as many as 500,000 births among adolescents each year in the United States.

Similarly, students should receive training in the practical aspects of parenthood. Relevant topics would include the fundamentals of child care, (e.g., feeding and changing a baby, nutrition, etc.), child management techniques and an understanding of the normal stages of human cognitive and physical development. The curriculum could also include techniques for helping all students better handle stressful situations, as well as strategies for enhancing communication between themselves and their family members. Of course, more and more schools are trying to offer courses and preparation in human relations skills and we think this is a very valuable thing to do. However, few schools provide specific instruction and practice in child care. Schools could provide practical experience in child care by giving older students the opportunity to work with children in community day care or preschool centers for credit. Such facilities often need volunteers and represent a virtually untapped resource available to educators for "parenthood training" for students. In addition, such volunteer efforts can provide a real contribution to the community, as well as child management experience for students. As many educators will attest, teenagers often have an idyllic view of marriage and family with little clear understanding of the rights and responsibilities of parenthood. Many believe that having a child will remedy a problem marriage. Providing teenagers with the opportunity for regular, supervised contact with children (perhaps in the context of a day care unit at school) will give them realistic experience in dealing with children. Remember, one of the best ways to interrupt the patterns of maltreatment is by teaching future parents the child care skills they need.

Finally, this educational program should include a consideration of the rights and obligations of children. There is a tendency in society to mistakenly view children as somehow exempt from certain legal and moral considerations afforded to adults. The realization that children also have the right to be respected as persons, have privacy, humane treatment, etc. may help to eliminate some of the excesses of parenting.

Continuing Education: Programs for Parents in the Community

Training in coping with the problems of family life should also be a service made available through community education to all adults who indicate an interest. Many parents, particularly new ones whose children are not yet of school age, would be grateful for the opportunity for adult education in parenting. Offering such a curriculum to parents in the community is well within the capabilities of the school, with flexible scheduling of classes to accomodate the work schedules of parents.

Community education in parenting could include some of the same areas already mentioned (i.e., nutrition, hygiene, birth control, human development, etc.) as well as some specialized areas. For example, many parents are anxious to learn home teaching techniques in reading, math and related areas in order to prepare their children for school or to help their children once they are in school. Many parents also wish to learn how to deal with sex education in the home. These sessions should also convey ideas for fostering better parent-child relations in general. Some parents are in need of learning how to cope with and resolve family conflicts by means other than through physical or psychological coercion. To the extent that interpersonal violence may have been learned as a vehicle for raising children, learning how to manage children without undesirable forms of punishment would be appropriate. Parents should also be taught how to effectively reduce acts of violence between siblings.

In addition, it is important to teach and foster an understanding of sex roles and sex role stereotypes. Parents should learn to view each child in his or her own right. The inability of children to meet unreasonable or conflicting expectations, (e.g., compulsive masculinity or femininity) can be a significant factor contributing to their maltreatment. Likewise, parents need to learn that many child rearing tasks should not be differentiated according to the sex of the parent. Nearly all parental role responsibilities should be mutually agreed upon and shared. Indeed, some research suggests that in households where there is a balance of power and shared child care responsibilities between parents, the likelihood of violence is reduced (Gelles, 1979). Above all, parents need to learn ways of establishing positive, intimate, communicative relationships with mates and children. Some persons who are unable to build satisfying emotional relationships resort to abuse in times of stress.

Another area in which schools could contribute to parent education is by developing special educational materials and programs for parents of impaired or otherwise exceptional children. Such children often require specialized care that some untrained parents may not be able to offer. Inability to provide this care or to cope with the frustrations engendered therein can lead to neglect or even physical abuse. Given that schools have access to trained personnel with the requisite skill and expertise in special education, considerable effort could be given to develop basic skills among these parents and to deflate the sense of futility and shame they experience.

Educating the Educators

Unfortunately, some school and agency personnel are no more informed about the nature of child abuse and neglect than the public they serve. And, of course, there are large numbers of professionals who need to know more in order to adequately do what they can to prevent abuse and neglect. Thus, in-service programs designed to enhance professional skills are crucial to prevention efforts. This can be accomplished by conducting a series of seminars or in-service workshops on various aspects of the problem, perhaps at the start of each school year. Legal, medical, social service and educational groups could each contribute to developing and conducting training sessions. The aid of experts in the local community—expert physicians, lawyers, agency heads, etc.—could be enlisted as key speakers. Such workshops are especially important to young teachers who may be less experienced in dealing with the problem. There is little doubt that if school accreditation were contingent upon developing policies and programs on child abuse, school personnel would pursue an even more active role in dealing with the problem.

Local colleges should also be encouraged to integrate material on child abuse and neglect into regular teacher training programs. One strategy schools could employ to affect colleges of education is to insist on hiring only those teachers who have gone through pre-service training programs in child abuse and neglect. Such an employment procedure costs a school district nothing yet can be effective in encouraging child abuse curriculum development in colleges and universities. The overall content of a teacher development program at both the pre-service and in-service levels could include discussions of the following topics:

1) legal rights and obligations;
2) social and physical characteristics associated with abuse and abusers;
3) reporting procedures;
4) appropriate community agencies and their functions;
5) practical aspects of case management and follow-up procedures;
6) strategies for working with parents and children;
7) problem areas in service delivery and ways to overcome these obstacles;
8) stress management and crisis intervention; and
9) children's rights and the problems of being a parent;

VOLUNTEER TRAINING PROGRAMS

Not only should school districts facilitate in-service and pre-service training programs for teachers and other school personnel, but programs should also be developed for school volunteers. Many interested citizens in the community could, with a modicum of training, provide considerable assistance to parents, service agencies and educators. These volunteers could serve professionals in a supportive capacity, especially in the areas of providing emergency shelter and home-maker assistance. Schools could help recruit and train neighborhood volunteers willing to serve as parent aides. These are lay people who, under child protective services' supervision, could make home visits, assist in child care and help provide emotional support to "high risk" parents. Not only would these aides help to relieve some of the stresses that can lead to abuse, but their presence would provide a stable model for "normal" behavior. Schools could also locate volunteers (perhaps from PTA groups) willing to provide emergency shelter and assist in crisis nurseries or day care centers. Volunteers could also be recruited to man the "hot lines" and serve as reference agents for community services.

Because schools often represent a focal point for neighborhood activities with contacts throughout the community, they have a tremendous potential for recruitment and training of persons able to act in a supportive capacity. All too often, the potential contributions of church groups, retired citizens, college students and others are not realized because there is no mechanism to encourage their involvement. The schools, in collaboration with service organizations, could train volunteers to help meet the unique needs of each community.

Preparing school staff agency personnel and community volunteers to respond to the various contingencies that may arise in cases of abuse and neglect is one of the strongest contributions schools can make to prevention efforts. A list of resource materials for possible use in inservice and pre-service training programs is provided in *Appendix H.*

Raising Community Awareness

Among the most challenging of all prevention goals is to create awareness in the community that a problem exists and that there are resources to deal with the problem. Equally difficult, once there is this general awareness, is to foster a broad commitment to solving the problem. Schools, in collaboration with local service agencies and volunteers, can employ a number of strategies to meet these goals which we have already discussed. However, there are a number of things that can be added here concerning how to build community awareness.

To begin, a public education campaign is not likely to be successful unless it addresses the subjective aspects of the problem. In other words, it is important to make people in the community feel that they are in some way affected by the condition and that something can be done about it. Unfortunately, many people view child abuse and neglect as a private problem rather than a public concern. Thus, there is a tendency to be acquiescent. One way to make the issue subjectively real to the public is to objectively demonstrate the tremendous cost involved, both financial and in terms of human suffering.

Disseminating child abuse and neglect information can be accomplished in several ways. One approach is to print and distribute pamphlets and posters throughout the community. This could be expedited by enlisting the aid of volunteer groups (e.g., Boy Scouts, Girl Scouts, church groups, etc.) to assist in distribution. A series of letters, editorials and advertisements in the local newspaper would also help generate attention. Book markers and match-books with hot line numbers could be distributed as well. Likewise, many radio and television stations are willing to provide free broadcast time for public service announcements. The main focus of this public awareness program is to get community members to realize a problem exists, to help them identify the symptoms and encourage them to report suspected cases of abuse and neglect to the proper authorities.

A word of caution must be made, however, when attempting to raise public awareness and involve the community. It is important to bring attention to the issue of child abuse and neglect in such a way that abusive parents and abused children are not stigmatized. The message should be conveyed that these are people in need of help and understanding rather than punishment and scorn. Child maltreatment is not really a "sickness" subject to one treatment, but a complex behavioral pattern that is embedded in both environmental and personality factors. To unintentionally evoke public condemnation toward individuals (rather than toward the situation itself) may make the problem worse. A public awareness program should be a "public education campaign" that promotes greater understanding in the community without stigmatizing the individuals affected.

As part of the effort to raise community consciousness, schools could sponsor an occasional open forum or
chautauqua on child abuse and neglect. Values clarifica-
tion, especially with respect to child rearing responsibilities
and the societal norms which legitimatize selective violence, should be among the central themes. These discussions should also include a consideration of possible
catalysts for violence (e.g., alcohol, unemployment,
marital tensions, violence in the media, etc.) as well as
ways the community can neutralize the pernicious effects
of these conditions.

Admittedly, efforts to raise community awareness may
do relatively little in terms of primary prevention. Perhaps
the main value of such efforts is in the area of secondary
prevention. By keeping the public informed, it is hoped
that there will be an increase in the rate of reporting and
self-referral, better utilization of existing services, increased recruitment of volunteers and ultimately an improvement in the quality of family life.

Additional Support Services for Prevention

Another area in which schools can contribute to the
prevention of child abuse and neglect is in the realm of
health. Each school could co-sponsor with their local
health department medical exams for all students and
check for signs of potential as well as actual abuse or

neglect as part of the exam. In addition, schools could assist child protective services staff by using volunteers to contact private physicians and hospital staff to make certain they are aware of referral procedures and the services provided to families by various agencies. Nagi (1977) indicates that medical personnel are relatively unaware of service groups (e.g., Parents Anonymous, Family and Children's Services, etc.) in the community and how they function. Perhaps some physicians view child maltreatment as a strictly medical rather than social problem. By keeping medical staff informed, it is hoped that there will be an increase in reporting and better use of available social services.

Schools can make several other contributions to prevention by offering services not typically associated with education. For example, a contingency fund providing emergency loans or clothing could be established to help alleviate stressful family situations. Although many schools are doing this now, this role could be expanded, especially with the aid of local service clubs. At any rate, the success of prevention efforts is likely to be enhanced if the schools, through their programs, can maintain high visibility and establish a broad basis of support in the community.

There is no empirical evidence that corporal punishment in schools is more effective than alternative methods. Indeed, the physical pain and the psychological degradation associated with physically coercive means of controlling children can result in the opposite of what is intended: a rejection of authority, a deep resentment of the school, and a continuation of rebellious behavior. The impact of this can be devastating to the learning environment.

By utilizing corporal punishment in school, an important social message is transmitted to all children: inducing physical pain is perceived as a legitimate and rational means of resolving conflict or modifying behavior. In an already violent society, should schools model & "legitimize" physical aggression? What are the long term consequences? Schools should take the lead in demonstrating that conflict can be resolved without the use of physical force.

Given that child abuse is often a "hidden crime," employing corporal punishment in school may inadvertently result in children who are already abused at home being subject to more physical coercion in school. The risk of this is significant when one considers that abused children often "act out" in school. Although corporal punishment might be effective in achieving temporary control, the long-term effects of this form of "motivation" are suspect, especially when the recipient is already the target of excessive punishment at home. The consequences of this are to reinforce violent behavioral patterns that are likely to persist into adult life. Perhaps this is why the American Psychological Association's council of representatives has opposed the use of corporal punishment.

SUGGESTED READINGS

Daniel, J. H., Newberger, D. H., Reed, R. B. and Kotel-
chuck, M., CHILD ABUSE SCREENING: IMPLICA-
TIONS OF THE LIMITED PREDICTIVE POWER
OF ABUSE DISCRIMINANTS FROM A CONTROL-
LED FAMILY STUDY OF PEDIATRIC SOCIAL
ILLNESS. Society for Research in Child Development
Biennial Meeting, New Orleans, LA, March 19, 1977.

Gelles, Richard J., FAMILY VIOLENCE. Beverly Hills,
CA: Sage Publications, 1979.

Meier, J.H., SYMPOSIUM ON PREVENTION: HELP-
ING PARENTS PARENT. In: Proceedings of the
First National Conference on Child Abuse and Neglect,
Regional Institute of Social Welfare Research, Athens,
GA, (OHD) 77-30094, 1977.

Plummer, Carol, PREVENT SEXUAL ABUSE. Holmes
Beach, FL: Learning Publications, Inc., 1984.

11

Programming for Teenage Parents

Teenage pregnancy is not an uncommon phenomenon in America. During the 1970s, the number of pregnancies increased among teenagers in all age-groups, and now exceeds 1 million a year. Projections by the Alan Guttmacher Institute indicate that if there is no change in current rates, four out of 10 girls who are now age 14 will get pregnant in their teens, with two in 10 giving birth, and three in 20 electing abortions (Alan Guttmacher Institute, 1981). Moreover, the younger the teenager, the most likely she will give birth to an unwanted child born out-of-wedlock (Phipps-Yonas, 1980). Nonetheless, it is estimated that ninety-six percent of unmarried teenage mothers keep their children (Alan Guttmacher Institute, 1981). For many of these teenagers, parenting will not be a joyful and rewarding experience. Indeed, research suggests that they are more likely than others to eventually abuse or neglect their children (Howard, 1978).

CONTRIBUTING FACTORS

It is not difficult to recognize some of the reasons why school-age parents run a high risk of becoming child abusers or of contributing to child neglect. Teenage parents are very likely to find themselves in stress situations which tax their ability to cope with the demands and responsibilities of child rearing. Chances are they will also face added stress associated with early and repeated pregnancies, single parenthood, unhappy early marriage, isolation from desired friends, handicapped children, limited awareness of how to effectively parent and poor relationships with their own parents.

Early and Repeated Pregnancies

Unfortunately, pregnancy among women under fifteen is on the increase. Evidence further indicates that as many as six out of every ten school-age mothers under sixteen will have another child while still of school age. To complicate matters, teenage mothers face stress brought on by the fact that their own physical and psychological development may still be incomplete.

If young parents are immature and insecure, they will find themselves faced with situations which require decision-making skills and mature judgement, neither of which they have had time to fully develop. As we have previously noted, some researchers suggest that immaturity contributes to a common set of behaviors exhibited by abusive parents and that this immaturity is related to unrealistic expectations of their children.

Single Parenthood

One of the most important and far-reaching social developments in America today is the single-parent family. Teenage mothers are a conspicuous segment of this type of family arrangement. In 1981, for example, more than half of the 1.3 million children who were living with teenage parents lived in households with unmarried mothers (Alan Guttmacher Institute, 1981). Moreover, because of the high divorce rate among teenagers, their children's chances of spending a large part of childhood in one parent families is much greater than that of their peers born to older women. Even if the father is present, the pressures placed on such young parents may give rise to abusive patterns. Almost inevitably, young, single parents experience considerable criticism and penalty. Furthermore, young people often lack the most basic economic and social support services to be effective parents.

Unhappy Marriages

When a single teenager gets pregnant, the parents may panic and pressure their child into a forced marriage. When this occurs, it often yields nothing but frustration and unhappiness for all the parties concerned. A predictable consequence may be an early divorce. Divorce among teenagers occurs at a rate three to four times higher than for any other age group. This can lead to social isolation from friends and family and produce considerable stress since fewer adults are available to help with the heavy demands of child raising.

Isolation From Peers

A young women who has a child may also find herself isolated from her former friends and school-mates. This is more likely to occur if she drops out of school. Unfortunately, pregnancy is still the leading cause of school drop-outs among young women. On the other hand, even if she stays in school, as a young mother, she is still likely to experience some pain, frustration and embarrassment often traced to discriminatory policies and practices. For example, she may be excluded from participation in extra-curricular activities and find no adequate substitute provisions for help.

Physically and Mentally Impaired Children

Research clearly indicates that pregnant teenagers are more likely than women in their twenties to give birth to infants who will have life-long handicaps such as hyper-kinesis, language delays, motor and mental impairment, and academic achievement problems (Anastasiow et. al. 1982). Tragically, the risk is greatest among mothers 15 and younger, an age-group presently experiencing the greatest increase in pregnancy and live-births (Campbell, 1980). Since difficulties associated with meeting the special needs of impaired children severely challenge the coping abilities of even the most secure and mature adults, it is predictable that teenage parents will be especially hard pressed to cope with them.

Limited Parenting Knowledge

Today's school age parent also runs the risk of knowing very little about child rearing and parenting responsibilities. The decline of the extended family, the decreased birth rate, changing parental and social arrangements and the isolation experienced by many families may account for this. Without appropriate role models from whom to learn, teenage parents are likely to enter adolescence and parenthood unprepared. A consequence is that they may be unable to provide proper care and nurture for their offspring and suffer further erosion of their self-images.

Faulty Parent-Child Interaction Systems

Research also shows that the younger the mother, the greater the chance of suffering a difficult pregnancy and having a low-birth weight and/or premature infant (Anastasiow, 1982). When this happens, early separation between the mother and child is likely to occur. This physical separation, some have argued, may retard and interrupt the "bonding" process between parent and infant—a process which may be critical to the development of a healthy parent-child relationship.

Financial Insecurity

Statistics also indicate that a large proportion of school-age parents face the prospect of depending on some sort of welfare in order to support themselves and their children. If they dropout of school, they will probably be lacking in the development of adequate work skills or work experience. Furthermore, even if they do find employment the pay will probably be low, making it difficult to obtain adequate childcare while at work. Socially isolated, teenage parents generally find little help in caring for their children. A consequence may be that they are trapped in a state of welfare dependency, an existence fraught with difficulties and stress producing situations.

Of course, we recognize that many teenagers are good parents despite the circumstances they face. Being a teenage parent does not automatically lead to child abuse or neglect. Educators should do all they can to discourage such stereotypes. However, as most educators already know, the challenges of parenthood tend to be compounded if one is very young, financially insecure and cut off from family and peer social supports. Unfortunately, the demands of parenthood and the social stigma associated with teenage parenthood can exascerbate the situation, with child mistreatment being the final result.

In summary, school-age mothers and fathers are vulnerable to becoming abusive or neglectful of their children unless given the proper training and support. They are more likely than older parents to exhibit behaviors and face circumstances which correlate highly with what we know about parents who abuse or neglect their children. Recall that they have a higher probability than most adults for abuse and neglect which is: 1) directly or indirectly related to poor self-images, immaturity and unfulfilled social and economic needs, and 2) having a child whom they perceive as different—who fails to respond as they desire or who is really "different" in that he or she may be mentally impaired, or suffering from a birth defect of some kind, etc. When these factors are accompanied by a crisis—minor or major—an explosion in violence can be triggered. Sometimes it takes the form of striking out physically against the children. Other times parents simply withdraw, ignoring and neglecting their offspring. Fortunately, there are things that can be done to help young school-age parents to become less likely to abuse or neglect their children. In this regard, the school can be of considerable assistance.

A SCHOOL PARENTING PROGRAM
FOR TEENAGE PARENTS

Although today's pregnant high school girls are much more likely to remain in school during their pregnancies than did their counterparts in the past (Mott and Maxwell, 1981), pregnancy is still the most common reason given for girls failing to complete high school, with between 50 and 67 percent of female dropouts falling into this category (Phipps-Yonas, 1980). We have reviewed some of the compelling health, educational and social reasons why school districts should take steps to keep pregnant students and young mothers in school. It is now generally accepted that there are legal obligations which apply as well.

Legal Rights Related to Pregnancy

School policies and practices which exclude pregnant women and school-age mothers from regular attendance generally are based on the assumption that their presence is disruptive to the learning process and a threat to the moral development of other students. Although these fears appear to be widespread among parents and school officials alike, recent court decisions suggest that such fears are not sufficient grounds for denying these students an equal educational opportunity. A case in point is the 1971 precedent setting decision of *Ordway v. Hargraves* in which an unmarried pregnant senior at North Middlesex Regional High School in Townsend, Massachusetts brought suit against the school district when she was excluded from regular class attendance by school officials.

The U.S. District Court (Mass.) found no compelling reason to uphold the school's decision to remove Ms. Ordway. Testimony by a physician indicated that there were no valid health reasons to warrant her exclusion. A psychiatrist testified that such an action could cause mental anguish which would negatively affect the course of her pregnancy. The Court concluded that the argument that her presence would disrupt and interfere with the school's ability to carry out its function was not justified by the facts presented. Consequently, the Court ordered that Ms. Ordway be readmitted to regular classes, be allowed to participate in extra-curricular activities and be kept on the school register until graduation (Fischer and Schimmel, 1982).

Educators should also be aware that under Title IX of the *Education Amendments of 1972* which forbids discrimination on the basis of sex, provision is made to protect the rights of young pregnant women and mothers. Any school receiving federal funds shall not: a) apply any rule concerning a student's actual or potential parental, family or marital status which treats students differently on the basis of sex; and b) discriminate against any student, or exclude any student from its education program or activity on the basis of such student's pregnancy or pregnancy-related condition (Goldmeier, 1976). School officials should not arbitrarily assign these young women to separate programs. Any program for pregnant students must be comparable to that offered non-pregnant students (Goldmeier, 1976) and must be compatible with the legal rights of these students.

The Nature of Parenting Education

If school districts are to meet the legal, professional and moral obligations of providing these young women an equal educational opportunity, they will have to provide learning experiences specifically designed to meet their special needs. Parenting education clearly addresses one of their most pressing and immediate needs.

Parenting education for all youth is seldom an integral part of a public school program. Reluctance to place this responsibility on the schools, the increased attention of late to return schools to the "basics" and the scarcity of dollars in many school districts to fund even existing programs help to explain why. There is evidence, however, that more emphasis and resources are being given to making it available to high risk teenagers—especially pregnant women and mothers — than was previously the case (Harrison, 1972; Jordon, 1978).

Nonetheless, other studies suggest that many schools neither seek nor want an active role in dealing with student pregnancy or parenthood (Zellman, 1982).

Parenting education has been defined (McAfee and Nedler, 1976) as any type of educaitonal program, involvement or intervention designed to increase parental competence and self-esteem in the parenting role. When directed at pregnant teenagers and young mothers, it is primarily aimed at realizing three goals (Howard, 1971):

1) to increase the chances of normal pregnancy and childbirth and to protect the health of both mother and infant;

2) to help young school-age parents solve the personal problems that may have led to their pregnancy or resulted from it and to direct them toward a satisfying future; and

3) to help young school-age parents continue their education before and after childbirth.

Making Contact

A school committed to helping any of its high risk students can only do so if it takes steps to identify those in need. The school staff should be on the alert for signs which suggest pregnancy and take the initiative to investigate pregnancy rumors in a discrete and professional manner. If a case is confirmed, every effort should be made to bring the young woman and, if appropriate, the father into contact with trained professionals who can assist them in dealing with likely difficulties. Making them aware of the range of educational, social and medical services available in the school and larger community will be valuable information for them whether they are married or not. Furthermore, by maintaining a non-judgemental attitude, the staff can create a climate of trust and acceptance which will communicate to them that there are people who care and are willing and able to help them during such trying times.

A well planned outreach system can bring young parents who have already dropped out of school back into contact with their high school and enable them to benefit from its parenting program. There are serious obstacles, however, which limit participation. One that usually faces young unmarried mothers is the need to care for the child while lacking the support of adults who could free her long enough to attend classes.

While lack of child care facilities can interfere and reduce the effectiveness of special programs for these high risk parents, school officials should not decide to cancel or curtail such programs. There are ways to combat the problem. One way would be the creation of an infant day care component where infants are given shelter and care during the school day. Such a component could be incorporated into a parenting program. There is solid evidence to suggest (Howard, 1971; Goldmeier, 1976) that if schools also make these services available to pregnant women, they will stay in school after giving birth. Schools may wish to explore the extent to which federal and state financial aid is available for such a program.

Housing The Students

Since the regular school is often perceived by pregnant students as a hostile environment in which they are the brunt of cruel jokes and subjected to social ostracism, school districts should give serious consideration to creating special programs for them. These programs may be housed in the same high school or may be conducted in a building exclusively given over for this purpose. Such an arrangement could protect from further damage the fragile self-images of many of these students. However, every effort should be made to not use special programming as a vehicle to segregate teenage mothers from others. If segregation is imposed for some reason, then making the total school a less hostile environment should still be an objective. If circumstances make complete integration impossible, teenage parents should be incorporated into the regular program as much as possible with provision made to meet any special needs they may have.

Transportation Needs

A major deterrent to school attendance by many pregnant young women and young mothers will simply be their inability to get to school. Providing transportation, therefore, becomes a condition which must be met if a district truly wants to develop a successful parenting program for them.

Comprehensive Services

When young school-age pregnant women are treated as high-risk patients and are provided comprehensive health services, their chances and the chances of their infants becoming victims of pregnant-related illness and

The Importance of Proper Nutrition

Research indicates that proper nutrition is one of the most important factors in a normal pregnancy (Anastasiow et. al. 1982). Being a growing teenager as well as being pregnant poses even more serious nutritional needs. Unfortunately, many pregnant young women suffer from poor eating habits which, if allowed to go uncorrected, become formidable health hazards. Shwedel, for example, has documented that low birth weight is linked to nutrition (Anastasiow et. al. 1982). Moreover, many young teenage parents-to-be will come from difficult home situations in which proper nutrition is neither consistently practiced nor well understood. Consequently, in-school educational programs for pregnant teenagers ought to include a nutritional component which informs about proper nutrition, promotes good nutritional habits, and provides for their nutritional needs through well-planned meals. Such an arrangement can serve a dual purpose: providing needed nutrition and becoming an activity around which proper nutrition for children is taught and reinforced.

Staffing and Their Responsibilities

In brief, parenting education for pregnant young women and teenage parents attempts to meet their medical care or related health needs, as well as their social and educational needs. This means that when assembling a school staff, an effort must be made to select professionals trained and competent in these areas of specialty.

The medical care/health specialist will generally be a school nurse, or a public health nurse, trained in maternity and infant care. His or her responsibilities may include offering instruction in: prenatal care; child birth; child rearing; family life and family planning (see *Figure 10.1* which offers a source of curriculum materials). With consent, the nurse can also maintain contact with physicians and assist in monitoring student progress during and after their pregnancies. If necessary, the nurse can conduct home visits and provide health care counseling with the young women's parents.

The social/psychological specialist may be a school counselor, psychologist or social worker. In fortunate situations where adequate personnel are available, the program may have all types of professional services. However, the major responsibilities of the social/psychological specialist, regardless of professional identities, is to help young parents cope with their personal problems during and after the pregnancy. Developing coping skills and interpersonal relations skills is emphasized. A guidance function should also be provided since the student is involved in completing academic and other studies as part of the overall program. Once the young mother has delivered and returns to the regular program to complete her studies, guidance and counseling services should be continued. If appropriate, these services could be made available to the father as well. When necessary, home visits should be made to help young parents cope with family problems that can be detrimental to pregnancy and their ability to complete the parenting program.

The educational specialists must ensure that the young parents or parents-to-be keep up with their classmates in the regular school. They can provide instruction during the time the young woman is in attendance in any special programs. Because of the nature of the special programs— the young women come in for varying lengths of time and their needs change depending upon whether they are pregnant or a mother with an infant in the day care component—the instructional methods must be flexible and highly individualized. It should go without saying that both these young women and the fathers, if present, should receive instruction in home making and family living.

The day care component may be crucial to the success of a program for teenage parents. It enables teenage parents to attend school because trained professionals and supportive staff are available to care for their infants while they attend class. It also enables the staff to better help each parent—those young parents who are expecting and those whose children are in day care—develop the knowledge and the attitudes fundamental to a proper parent-child relationship.

A word of çaution. Although parenting education is receiving recognition as a potentially viable strategy aimed at preventing child abuse and neglect, to-date there is little hard evidence to warrant any final conclusions as to its effectiveness in this regard (McAfee and Nedler, 1976). One area of concern is that little attention is paid to males and young fathers in existing parenting education programs (Robinson and Barret, 1982). When it is directed at high risk young women, it seems reasonable to expect some positive effects since emphasis is placed not only on transmitting information but also on preventing circumstances from emerging which have been linked with abuse and neglect. But such optimism must be tempered by the realization that there are many variables which lie outside the control of the school that help to shape their lives. And like it or not, they often determine the degree of success of the school's effort.

PROGRAMMING FOR TEENAGE PARENTS

1) **Project FEED** (Facilitative Environments Encouraging Development), 1981. Developed by the Institute for Child Study, Indiana University, Bloomington, Indiana. (Materials now distributed by Educational Development Center, 55 Chapel Street, Newton, Mass. 02160).

Description

Project FEED is a preparent education program designed for middle school students (grades 6 thru 8) but flexible enough to be used with high school age students. The goals of the program are to: 1) help students develop knowledge and understandings in the area of child development, 2) equip students with essential child care skills, and 3) nurture positive attitudes toward parenting and children. Students who participate in the program can develop and apply learnings in four possible settings: 1) a traditional classroom setting, 2) a normal preschool setting, 3) a handicapped setting, and 4) a medical or health-related setting. The *Curriculum Guide* developed by Project FEED's staff contains a list of objectives along with sample lesson plans, bibliography and useful teaching aids. School personnel implementing the program can select from 33 objectives those which best meet the needs of their students. The design of the program allows for a variety of instructional arrangements, including instruction for 9-, 16-, and 36-week programs.

2) **Young, Single and Pregnant: A New Perspective**

Four parts, 10-13 minutes each, filmstrips and cassettes; slides; video cassettes, U Matic, Beta, or VHS. Guidance Associates Inc., Box 3000, Mount Kisco, NY 10549.

Description

This program is an excellent resource for helping students understand the causes and consequences of teenage pregnancy. A case studies approach is used in the series thereby enabling students to apply newly acquired information to real-life problems and concerns. The accompanying *Teacher's Guide* provides a variety of discussion questons and group oriented activities aimed at engaging students in a critical and reflective examination of their own sexual attitudes and preferences. The program stresses prevention as a goal.

SUGGESTED READINGS

Anastasiow, Nicholas J., et. al., THE ADOLESCENT PARENT. Baltimore: Paul H. Brookes Publishing Co., 1982.

Darabi, Katherine F., "A Closer Look At Schooling After the First Birth." JOURNAL OF SCHOOL HEALTH, March 1982, Vol. 52, No. 3

McQuiston, M., "Crisis Nurseries." In: H. P. Martin (Ed.), THE ABUSED CHILD: A MULTIDISCIPLINARY APPROACH TO DEVELOPMENTAL ISSUES AND TREATMENT. Cambridge, Massachusetts: Ballinger Publishing Co., 1976.

National Federation of Settlements and Neighborhood Centers. EDUCATION FOR PARENTHOOD PROGRAMS. Final Report: DHEW, 1976.

Smith, Peggy B., Weinman, Maxine L., and Mumford, David M., "Social and Affective Factors Associated with Adolescent Pregnancy." THE JOURNAL OF SCHOOL HEALTH, February 1982, Vol. 52, No. 2.

APPENDICES

Appendix A:
FEDERAL LEGISLATION

Public Law 93–247
93rd Congress, S. 1191
January 31, 1974

An Act

To provide financial assistance for a demonstration program for the prevention, identification, and treatment of child abuse and neglect, to establish a National Center on Child Abuse and Neglect, and for other purposes.

Be it enacted by the Senate and House of Representatives of the United States of America in Congress assembled, That this Act may be cited as the "Child Abuse Prevention and Treatment Act".

THE NATIONAL CENTER ON CHILD ABUSE AND NEGLECT

SEC. 2. (a) The Secretary of Health, Education, and Welfare (hereinafter referred to in this Act as the "Secretary") shall establish an office to be known as the National Center on Child Abuse and Neglect (hereinafter referred to in this Act as the "Center").

(b) The Secretary, through the Center, shall—

(1) compile, analyze, and publish a summary annually of recently conducted and currently conducted research on child abuse and neglect;

(2) develop and maintain an information clearinghouse on all programs, including private programs, showing promise of success, for the prevention, identification, and treatment of child abuse and neglect;

(3) compile and publish training materials for personnel who are engaged or intend to engage in the prevention, identification, and treatment of child abuse and neglect;

(4) provide technical assistance (directly or through grant or contract) to public and nonprofit private agencies and organizations to assist them in

planning, improving, developing, and carrying out programs and activities relating to the prevention, identification, and treatment of child abuse and neglect;

    (5) conduct research into the causes of child abuse and neglect, and into the prevention, identification, and treatment thereof; and

    (6) make a complete and full study and investigation of the national incidence of child abuse and neglect, including a determination of the extent to which incidents of child abuse and neglect are increasing in number or severity.

(c) The Secretary may carry out his functions under subsection (b) of this section either directly or by way of grant or contract.*

DEFINITION

SEC. 3. For purposes of this Act the term "child abuse and neglect" means the physical or mental injury, sexual abuse, negligent treatment, or maltreatment of a child under the age of eighteen by a person who is responsible for the child's welfare under circumstances which indicate that the child's health or welfare is harmed or threatened thereby, as determined in accordance with regulations prescribed by the Secretary.

DEMONSTRATION PROGRAMS AND PROJECTS

SEC. 4. (a) The Secretary, through the Center, is authorized to make grants to, and enter into contracts with, public agencies or nonprofit private organizations (or combinations thereof) for demonstration programs and projects designed to prevent, identify, and treat child abuse and neglect. Grants or contracts under this subsection may be—

    (1) for the development and establishment of training programs for professional and paraprofessional personnel in the fields of medicine, law, education, social work, and other relevant fields who are engaged in, or intend to work in, the field of the prevention, identification, and treatment of child abuse and neglect; and training programs for children, and for persons responsible for the welfare of children, in methods of protecting children from child abuse and neglect;

    (2) for the establishment and maintenance of centers, serving defined geographic areas, staffed by multidisciplinary teams of personnel trained in the prevention, identification, and treatment of child abuse and neglect cases, to provide a broad range of services related to child abuse and neglect, including direct support and supervision of satellite centers and attention homes, as well as providing advice and consultation to individuals, agencies, and organizations which request such services;

(3) for furnishing services of teams of professional and paraprofessional personnel which are trained in the prevention, identification, and treatment of child abuse and neglect cases, on a consulting basis to small communities where such services are not available; and

(4) for such other innovative programs and projects, including programs and projects for parent self-help, and for prevention and treatment of drug-related child abuse and neglect, that show promise of successfully preventing or treating cases of child abuse and neglect as the Secretary may approve.

Not less than 50 per centum of the funds appropriated under this Act for any fiscal year shall be used only for carrying out the provisions of this subsection.

(b) (1) Of the sums appropriated under this Act for any fiscal year, not less than 5 per centum and not more than 20 per centum may be used by the Secretary for making grants to the States for the payment of reasonable and necessary expenses for the purpose of assisting the States in developing, strengthening, and carrying out child abuse and neglect prevention and treatment programs.

(2) In order for a State to qualify for assistance under this subsection, such State shall—

(A) have in effect a State child abuse and neglect law which shall include provisions for immunity for persons reporting instances of child abuse and neglect from prosecution, under any State or local law, arising out of such reporting;

(B) provide for the reporting of known and suspected instances of child abuse and neglect;

(C) provide that upon receipt of a report of known or suspected instances of child abuse or neglect an investigation shall be initiated promptly to substantiate the accuracy of the report, and, upon a finding of abuse or neglect, immediate steps shall be taken to protect the health and welfare of the abused or neglected child, as well as that of any other child under the same care who may be in danger of abuse or neglect;

(D) demonstrate that there are in effect throughout the State, in connection with the enforcement of child abuse and neglect laws and with the reporting of suspected instances of child abuse and neglect, such administrative procedures, such personnel trained in child abuse and neglect prevention and treatment, such training procedures, such institutional and other facilities (public and private), and such related multidisciplinary programs and services as may be necessary or appropriate to assure that the State will deal effectively with child abuse and neglect cases in the State;

(E) provide for methods to preserve the confidentiality of all records in order to protect the rights of the child, his parents or guardians;

(F) provide for the cooperation of law enforcement officials, courts of competent jurisdiction, and appropriate State agencies providing human services;

(G) provide that in every case involving an abused or neglected child which results in a judicial proceeding a guardian ad litem shall be appointed to represent the child in such proceedings;

(H) provide that the aggregate of support for programs or projects related to child abuse and neglect assisted by State funds shall not be reduced below the level provided during fiscal year 1973, and set forth policies and procedures designed to assure that Federal funds made available under this Act for any fiscal year will be so used as to supplement and, to the extent practicable, increase the level of State funds which would, in the absence of Federal funds, be available for such programs and projects;

(I) provide for dissemination of information to the general public with respect to the problem of child abuse and neglect and the facilities and prevention and treatment methods available to combat instances of child abuse and neglect; and

(J) to the extent feasible, insure that parental organizations combating child abuse and neglect receive preferential treatment.

(3) Programs or projects related to child abuse and neglect assisted under part A or B of title IV of the Social Security Act shall comply with the requirements set forth in clauses (B), (C), (E), and (F) of paragraph (2).

(c) Assistance provided pursuant to this section shall not be available for construction of facilities; however, the Secretary is authorized to supply such assistance for the lease or rental of facilities where adequate facilities are not otherwise available, and for repair or minor remodeling or alteration of existing facilities.

(d) The Secretary shall establish criteria designed to achieve equitable distribution of assistance under this section among the States, among geographic areas of the Nation, and among rural and urban areas. To the extent possible, citizens of each State shall receive assistance from at least one project under this section.

(e) For the purposes of this section, the term "State" includes each of the several States, the District of Columbia, the Commonwealth of Puerto Rico, American Samoa, the Virgin Island, Guam and the Trust Territories of the Pacific.*

AUTHORIZATIONS

SEC. 5. There are hereby authorized to be appropriated for the purposes of this Act $15,000,000 for the fiscal year ending June 30, 1974, $20,000,000 for the fiscal year ending June 30, 1975, and $25,000,000 for the fiscal year ending June 30, 1976, and for the succeeding fiscal year.

ADVISORY BOARD ON CHILD ABUSE AND NEGLECT

SEC. 6. (a) The Secretary shall, within sixty days after the date of enactment of this Act, appoint an Advisory Board on Child Abuse and Neglect (hereinafter referred to as the "Advisory Board"), which shall be composed of representatives from Federal agencies with responsibility for programs and activities related to child abuse and neglect, including the Office of Child Development, the Office of Education, the National Institute of Education, the National Institute of Mental Health, the National Institute of Child Health and Human Development, the Social and Rehabilitation Service, and the Health Services Administration. The Advisory Board shall assist the Secretary in coordinating programs and activities related to child abuse and neglect administered or assisted under this Act with such programs and activities administered or assisted by the Federal agencies whose representatives are members of the Advisory Board. The Advisory Board shall also assist the Secretary in the development of Federal standards for child abuse and neglect prevention and treatment programs and projects.

(b) The Advisory Board shall prepare and submit, within eighteen months after the date of enactment of this Act, to the President and to the Congress a report on the programs assisted under this Act and the programs, projects, and activities related to child abuse and neglect administered or assisted by the Federal agencies whose representatives are members of the Advisory Board. Such report shall include a study of the relationship between drug addiction and child abuse and neglect.

(c) Of the funds appropriated under section 5, one-half of 1 per centum, or $1,000,000, whichever is the lesser, may be used by the Secretary only for purposes of the report under subsection (b).

COORDINATION

SEC. 7. The Secretary shall promulgate regulations and make such arrangements as may be necessary or appropriate to ensure that there is effective coordination between programs related to child abuse and neglect under this Act and other such programs which are assisted by Federal funds.

Approved January 31, 1974.

*Amendments Section 2(c) and Section 4(e) added by P.L. 93-644, approved January 3, 1975.

LEGISLATIVE HISTORY:

HOUSE REPORT No. 93–685 (Comm. on Education and Labor).
SENATE REPORT No. 93–308 (Comm. on Labor and Public Welfare).
CONGRESSIONAL RECORD, Vol. 119 (1973):
    July 14, considered and passed Senate.
    Dec. 3, considered and passed House, amended.
    Dec. 20, Senate agreed to House amendments with amendments.
    Dec. 21, House concurred in Senate amendments.

Appendix B:
A SAMPLE SCHOOL POLICY

A POLICY STATEMENT
ON CHILD ABUSE AND NEGLECT:
DENVER, COLORADO PUBLIC SCHOOLS*

In accord with Colorado Statutes, Denver Public Schools has responsibilities in the area of child abuse. Both statutes and procedures have been revised several times since they were instituted in 1963. To clarify the roles and responsibilities of the school district and its personnel, the following sections of the law are stated:

Article 10 of Title 19, Colorado Revised Statutes 1973 as REPEALED AND REENACTED WITH AMENDMENTS, in 1975.

---

*This policy statement is one of several illustrations contained in Report No. 85 prepared by the Child Abuse and Neglect Project of the Education Commission of the States. The report is titled Education Policies and Practices Regarding Child Abuse and Neglect and Recommendations for Policy Development. Published in April, 1976, it was one of 16 resource projects by the National Center on Child Abuse and Neglect. The purpose of the report is "to offer guildelines to help education policy makers — from school principals to members of state boards of education — formulate child abuse policies."

19–10–103 DEFINITIONS

(1) (a) "Abuse" or "child abuse or neglect" means an act or omission in one of the following categories which seriously threatens the health or welfare of a child:

(I) Any case in which a child exhibits evidence of skin bruising, bleeding, malnutrition, failure to thrive, burns, fractures of any bone, subdural hematoma, soft tissue swelling, or death, and such condition or death is not justifiably explained, or where the history given concerning such condition or death, or circumstances indicate that such condition or death may not be the product of an accidental occurrence;

(II) Any case in which a child is subjected to sexual assault or molestation;

(III) Any case in which the child's parents, legal guardians, or custodians fail to take the same actions to provide adequate food, clothing, shelter, or supervision that a prudent parent would take.

19–10–104 PERSONS REQUIRED TO REPORT
CHILD ABUSE OR NEGLECT

(1) Any person specified in subsection (2) of this section who has reasonable cause to know or suspect that a child has been subjected to abuse or neglect or who has observed the child being subjected to circumstances or conditions which would reasonably result in abuse or neglect shall immediately report or cause a report to be made of such fact to the county department or local law enforcement agency.

(2)   Persons required to report such abuse or neglect or circumstances or conditions shall include any:

  (a) Physicians or surgeon, including a physician in training;
  (i) Registered nurse or licensed practical nurse;
  (l) School official or employee;
  (m) Social worker, or worker in a family care home or child care center, as defined in Section 26–6–102, C.R.S. 1973.

(4)   Any person who willfully violates the provisions of subsection (1) of this section:

  (a) Commits a class 2 petty offense and, upon conviction thereof, shall be punished by a fine not to exceed two hundred dollars;
  (b) Shall be liable for damages proximately caused thereby.

In Denver County, the implementation of this law is the responsibility of the Delinquency Control Division working in cooperation with the Division of Services for Families, Children and Youth of the Denver Department of Social Services.

To fulfill our obligations to our pupils in conformity with the law of the State, the following procedures have been developed:

  (1) When there is good reason to believe a child has been abused, the principal or his designee, after consultation with the social worker and the nurse, shall call the Police Dispatcher, 297–2011. The Dispatcher will wish to know the identity of the caller,

the location and the telephone number of the school, and the general nature of the complaint. A uniformed officer will respond within the shortest possible time. It is his responsibility, using whatever information the school nurse, the school social worker, teachers and other school personnel can supply him, to make an immediate judgment as to disposition. His alternatives are:

(a) Take the child to Denver General Hospital for medical examination.

(b) Take the child to the Delinquency Control Division for further questioning and possible placement outside the home.

(c) Take the child to his home himself.

(d) Leave the child in school.

(2) Whatever disposition the officer makes at the time, he is required immediately to file a report with DCD upon which an experienced detective will be assigned to make a thorough investigation.

Subsequent investigation and action to help prevent further physical abuse to the child are the responsibility of DCD working with the Department of Social Services. No one can remove a child from the home without police authority.

Every attempt should be made to preserve the best possible relationships between school and parents, since it is likely that the child will return to the home sooner or later and hence to school. The following policy applies to this situation.

"Denver Public School Policy 1206C
PUPILS, DISMISSAL OF DURING SCHOOL
SESSION

Section D — Custody requested by police offi-
cer. Whenever a police officer desires to take a
child into custody, the principal shall release
the child to the police officer and shall notify
the child's parents of his action. The police officer shall notify the principal of the specific
grounds for taking the child into temporary
custody. The principal shall advise the child's
parents of the grounds stated and shall note
this information on the notification memorandum. The principal, in all cases, should prepare
the notification memorandum (see attached
form). One copy should be maintained in the
school file and one copy should be sent to the
parents.

    Section E — The principal will make every
effort possible to insure that the taking of custody be made in privacy, preferably in the principal's office."

(3) The principal or his designee shall immediately
write a "Child Abuse Report." This form, CAR
975, is new and is available only through the Department of Health Services or the Department of
Social Work Services.

    Three copies of this form are to be filled out and
the original is to be mailed at once to the Division
of Services for Children and Youth, 456 Bannock

Street, 80204. One copy is attached to the child's
health record and the third copy goes to Health
Services for the central file.

(4)　In cases where long-standing abuse rather than
acute mistreatment is involved, i.e., those medically
diagnosed as "malnutrition" and "failure to thrive,"
form CAR 975 is to be written up and mailed as
above. It is not necessary, in such cases, to call the
Police Dispatcher.

　　　It might be helpful to consult with your School
Resource officer if you have questions. If you wish
to refer to the Denver Department of Social Services, please call Services for Children and Youth,
778–6363.

(5)　The above categories are clear and should be taken
care of promptly. Not so simple are cases of minimal damage. Often repeated instances of minor
contusions or the child's fearful (or angry) reports
are significant in a longitudinal study. Here also
may be an opportunity to do preventive work —
directly by the school team, referral to an appropriate agency, etc. Hopefully, personnel and parents
can be used and extended to serve the child's welfare. If, however, there is not improvement in the
situation, a report must be made with full docu-
mentation as to the methods the school has used in
attempting to better the child's condition.

(6)　Professional judgment must be brought to bear on
history and physical evidence in assessing the validity of a charge of child abuse. It is hoped that the
school nurse will have an opportunity to see each

child suspected of having been maltreated and that his/her opinion will be part of the evaluation. The Health Services Department physicians will be glad to give consultation if this is desired. The teacher and social worker usually have significant contributions to make.

(7) Remember that *any* citizen may report what he or she considers child abuse by calling the Police Dispatcher, 297-2011 or the Department of Families, Children and Youth Services, 778-6363. Anonymous as well as identified callers can be assured the complaint will be investigated. In general, the procedures which involve cooperative efforts of several staff members have been found to offer the best long-term program for the child's welfare.

The law specifically states (19-10-110) "Any person participating in good faith in the making of a report or in a judicial proceeding held pursuant to this title . . . shall be immune from any liability, civil or criminal, that otherwise might result by reasons of such reporting."

Comment

The difficult problem of developing a plan which will be most desirable for the welfare of the child takes the best efforts of many people. It is imperative that law enforcement, medical and social agencies share all available information and work together towards the best possible solution. While the welfare of the child is of primary concern, we must remember that parents have feelings and rights. The dependent child, himself, is torn between his loyalty to his family and his mental and physical suffering. Parents who abuse their children have serious family problems and need help and treatment for their own illness.

Our ultimate goal is a long-term one, expressed in the Colorado Children's Code as:

- To secure for each child such care and guidance, preferably in his own home, as will best serve his welfare and the interest of society.

- To preserve and strengthen family ties whenever possible, including improvement of the home environment.

Special Concerns of Health Services Department

The Health Services Department needs procedures for monitoring and evaluating the program. These include (1) preparation of reports at monthly intervals, (2) establishment of a central file of reported cases, and (3) follow-up information to indicate the outcome of the handling methods selected in individual cases. Each school should designate someone (probably the nurse or social worker) to inquire of the family, Division of Children and Youth Services, School Resource officer or other appropriate sources as to what happened as a result of the report. To implement these, after the report has been sent, we are asking the school nurse to:

(1) File a copy of form CAR 975 with the child's health record;

(2) Attach a copy of CAR 975 to the Monthly Report for the Health Services Department central file;

(3) Send follow-up information to Health Services Department. She will use "additional Pupil Health Information," Stock No. 01–0300.07, which will then be attached to the central file record. Appropriate comments should be added to the child's health record.

Special Concerns of Social Work Services

(1) Optimum school team involvement in preventive work with families who are having difficulties with their children and who may have problems in dealing with their frustrations.

This might include assessment of causes for a child's failure in the classroom, physical needs, and emotional and relationship problems. Such remedial measures as are possible in school should be provided. Perhaps the parents can be helped with disciplinary methods and in reinforcing the school's attempts toward better motivation of the child.

(2) Prompt and continued communication with other social agencies.

It would be helpful if the school social worker called Children and Youth Services immediately when a Child Abuse Report is made to determine what useful information the school may have regarding the child's social background and academic situation and how it may best be made available to those carrying responsibility for the case.

It is possible that not all information may be available to the school at the time when the report should be made. The report should not be delayed while the school social worker attempts to obtain any missing items. Send the report in immediately and the school social worker, with the Children and Youth worker, will determine how the remainder can best be obtained.

(3) An adequate compilation of social follow-up material to be supplied to the nurse for inclusion in the central file.

John M. Lampe, M.D., Executive Director
Department of Health Services

James M. O'Hara, Executive Director
Department of Pupil Services

Appendix C:
SAMPLE SCHOOL REPORT FORM

SAMPLE SCHOOL REPORT FORM
FOR CHILD ABUSE OR NEGLECT

Name of Child _____ Age _____
Child's Address _____ Sex _____
_____ Grade _____

Name of Parent(s) or Guardian(s)   Address   Phone
_____
_____

Type of Suspected Abuse or Neglect:
_____ Burns   _____ Sexual Abuse
_____ Beating   _____ Abandonment
_____ Fracture   _____ Malnutrition
_____ Neglect   _____ Other (specify) _____
_____
_____

Date of Suspected Incident _____

Statement of Time, Place and Conditions Prompting Report: _____
_____
_____
_____
_____
_____

_____

_____

Child's Account of Injury or Situation: _____

_____

_____

_____

_____

_____

Person or Agency Receiving Report: _____

_____

Measures (if any) Taken to Notify Parents or Guardians:

_____

_____

_____

Other Pertinent Information (e.g., relevant health information; knowledge of family situation; etc.): _____

_____

_____

_____

_____

_____

_____

Person Making Report:
Signature _____ Date _____
Title _____ Phone _____

Appendix D:
A FLOW CHART: AN ILLUSTRATION OF CHILD PROTECTIVE SERVICES

REPORT FROM SCHOOL

Building Child Abuse and Neglect (CAN) team reports the possibility of child maltreatment to the appropriate community agency.

INVESTIGATION

Appropriate community agency (e.g., Department of Human Services, Family and Children's Services, etc.) receives report and investigates case.

EVALUATION

Legal, educational, medical and mental health aspects of case are evaluated; a determination of abuse or neglect is made and the possibility of further risk is evaluated.

CASE CLOSED

Report of abuse or neglect not substantiated.

LOW RISK: HOME RELATIVELY SAFE

Services provided to parents and children.

HIGH RISK: HOME UNSAFE

Petition court to remove child from home.

EVALUATION & FOLLOW-UP CARE

Child left in parents' custody; therapy and support services for parents and children.

COURT DECISION

Child placed in a temporary or long-term foster care; therapy and support services for parents.

COMMUNITY SUPPORT GROUPS

Social service, school, medical and volunteer groups provide assistance.

EVALUATION AND FOLLOW-UP CARE

*A flow chart similar to the one above should be developed for each district and provided to all school staff.

Appendix E:
A SAMPLE CONTINUOUS FOLLOW-UP FORM FOR SCHOOLS

In Chapter 6, we stressed the need for a continued flow of information between the school and the community child protective services personnel after the initial report has been made. Such liason is essential in order to mark the progress of each case and provide the best school programming for the child. The school staff person who has responsibility for coordinating activities within a school should also have a continually developing record of all actions taken by school staff relevant to the status of the case. This record can be quickly shared with other school and child protective agency personnel as the case develops. The following is a sample follow-up form that schools may wish to employ as a means for grouping and sharing information.

FOLLOW-UP FORM

(Note: Recorders should initial and date all entries they make.)

Name of Child _____ Age _____
Child's Address _____ Sex _____
_____ Grade _____

Name of Parent(s) or Guardian(s)   Address   *Phone

_____

_____

Names of Others Living in Family (if any) / Relationship / Age

_____

_____

_____

_____

Statement of Time, Place and Conditions Prompting Initial Report: _____

_____

_____

_____

_____

_____

Current Behavioral Assessments of Child (e.g., child's academic performance; school attendance; child's relationship with peers and adults; with parents; etc.): _____

_____

_____

_____

_____

_____

Information Obtained From Protective Services & Other
Sources On Child: _____

_____

_____

_____

_____

_____

Types of Community Interventions, and By Whom (e.g.,
family counseling; foster care; court involvement; etc.):

_____

_____

_____

_____

Special Actions Taken by School on Behalf of Child:

_____

_____

_____

_____

Added Comments: _____

_____

_____

_____

_____

_____

_____

_____

_____

_____

Recorders:

_____
Signature   Title   Phone

_____
Signature   Title   Phone

_____
Signature   Title   Phone

_____
Signature   Title   Phone

_____
Signature   Title   Phone

_____
Signature   Title   Phone

Appendix F:
A SCHOOL'S REPONSE:
AN ILLUSTRATION

It is difficult to communicate the dynamics of various processes by which schools may respond to neglect or abuse by merely presenting policy suggestions. For this reason, we suggest that training programs develop problematic incidents and hypothetical responses to various types of maltreatment in order to better communicate possible solutions to the problem. In this appendix, an illustration of a hypothetical case of neglect is provided. Other hypothetical and actual illustrations of a variety of maltreatment situations should be developed for these training sessions.

A SCHOOL'S RESPONSE: AN ILLUSTRATION

Mr. Philips is a 4th grade teacher at Jackson, one of four elementary schools in Deerfield. He is a beginning teacher who has attended the district's child abuse and neglect workshops. He is confident that he knows what to look for and what to do if he is confronted by a child whose symptoms suggest possible or actual abuse and/or neglect.

A Problematic Incident

It is a cold, rainy Monday morning. As Mr. Philips drives into the school parking lot at 7:45 he notices a boy huddled in one of the doorways. Upon closer inspection he notices that the child is without a jacket and hat, is quite wet and is shivering. Shielding the boy with his umbrella, he grabs his hand and they make a dash for the front door.

Once inside, he finds out that the boy is Jody Williams, a 6th grader in Mrs. Fielding's room. He learns that Jody knows that students are not allowed in the building until 8:30 and are discouraged from arriving early on stormy days. He also learns that Jody left home without breakfast, a practice which he suspects is not uncommon in Jody's home. Jody is very reluctant to answer other questions so Mr. Philips takes him to his classroom, makes two cups of hot chocolate and allows Jody to help in setting up the overhead and slide projectors.

Later when Mrs. Fielding arrives, Mr. Philips escorts Jody to her room. Meeting with her in the hallway outside her classroom, Mr. Philips explains what has happened. Mrs. Fielding comments that for the past week or so Jody's behavior has deteriorated to a point where disciplinary action was necessary. Jody was kept after school on two occasions as a punishment. Much to the dismay of Mrs. Fielding, he seemed to enjoy this. She also indicates that Jody has a history of unruly behavior, tardiness and a level of absenteeism which she finds disturbing. This is the first time to her knowledge that a teacher has suspected possible physical and nutritional neglect.

In keeping with the district's child abuse and neglect policy, Mr. Philips asks to meet with the building principal at which time he orally reports the incident. The principal fills out the *Preliminary Child Abuse and Neglect Reporting Form* which calls for the name of the child, the name of the reporting teacher and the indicators which suggest possible abuse and/or neglect.

Convening the Child Abuse and Neglect Team

Immediately after receiving the report, the principal contacts the members of the school's Child Abuse and Neglect (CAN) Team. It consists of four persons — the school's social worker, school nurse, building principal, and the homeroom teacher of the child. The team is responsible for interviewing the child, rating the severity of the abuse and/or neglect, and selecting the appropriate course of action from among the existing list of alternatives previously worked out by the district's administrative staff in cooperation with the Child Protective Services Unit of the Department of Human Services.

Interviewing the Child

The interview is important in that it will enable the team to develop a profile of characteristics which will help define the nature and extent of Jody's maltreatment. This information will then become the basis by which the team decides which course of action to follow. However, even if the team concludes that the reported incident is a false alarm, a call is still made to the department of human services in order to comply with the state's law which requires professional educators to report all suspected or known cases of child abuse and neglect. By doing so, the principal protects himself against legal and criminal liability.

Generally, at Jackson only one team member conducts the interview. Consideration is given to selecting the person most likely to relate effectively with this particular child. Since probing into the child's family life can lead to an invasion of privacy, care is taken to avoid asking unnecessary and offensive questions. Sensitive to Jody's situation and experienced in matters relating to abuse and neglect, the interviewer consciously tries to reduce the anxiety associated with talking to a non-family member about family matters.

A set of *what to do* and *what not to do* guidelines are kept in mind prior to and during the interview. These include the following:

- Start the interview by first building a sense of trust and acceptance. Try to help the child relax. (Illustration: "Hi, Jody, Mr. Philips told me about your experience in the rain this morning. He said he hasn't run as fast since his college track days. He thinks you'll be a fine sprinter someday.")

- Avoid asking questions or making observations which place the child on the defensive. For example, do not begin by asking questions such as: "What did you do to *deserve* this treatment, Jody?"

- Explain that the purpose of the interview is to help not punish, the child or his family. (Illustration: "Jody, we are quite concerned about you. Coming to school without a jacket in weather like this could lead to a nasty cold or worse.")

- Avoid blaming the parents or implying that they are bad or unloving. (Illustration: "Loving parents don't mistreat their children. Are they always this mean to you?")

- Answer honestly the child's questions. (Illustration: "Yes, we will have to contact your parents about this so that they will become aware of our concern.")

- Avoid explanations which can be interpreted negatively by the child and which might frighten or alarm him unnecessarily. (Illustration: "Yes, sometimes children are removed from the home but we will have to learn more about your situation before we can decide if this applies to you.")

Rating the Severity of the Maltreatment

Once the interview is completed, the team meets to

discuss the findings. If the team decides the situation is of severe or moderate severity, the district policy is to let the department of human services handle it. The school's special services personnel can intervene on behalf of the child only after consultation with the assigned case worker. The school is not allowed in this instance to initiate action independently of the department but is encouraged to play a supportive role consistent with its educational responsibilities.

If the team concludes that the severity is mild or that the situation reflects potential for (but not actual) abuse or neglect, the district policy authorizes the school to intervene directly on behalf of the child. However, prior to initiating any plan of action, the team must inform the department of human services of its intentions, reach an agreement that the school's proposed plan of action is not in conflict with the department's mandated responsibilitiy and make arrangements whereby a case worker is made available to assist the school if and when necessary.

In Jody's case, the team first discusses the results of the interview and then reviews his cumulative folder for additional information which might shed further light on the incident.

Recommended Course of Action

After reviewing the situation, the team's primary conclusion is that Jody is a victim of neglect brought on by conditions relating to his mother's working schedule and pressures relating to single parenthood. To remedy the problem, the school's social worker and nurse will meet with Jody's mother and older sister to explain and impress upon them the relationship between proper sleep and diet and physical and educational growth. They will help them establish a set of reasonable rules for Jody to follow and will arrange for his homeroom teacher to monitor his progress and report any behaviors which suggest a possible relapse into his former patterns.

Armed with the information gathered from the interview and the team's conclusions and recommendations, the principal calls the department of human services. The department's intake unit listens to the account and indicates that the incident does not warrant assigning a specific case worker to investigate beyond what the school has already done. The department offers verbal support of the school's proposed plan of action and agrees to place a case worker on standby to assist the school if and when appropriate.

Next, the principal calls Jody's mother to explain what has happened and what response the staff proposes in order to help Jody cope more effectively with school. He also explains that in compliance with the state's child abuse and neglect law he has contacted the department of human services. He is careful to explain that the department does not view the situation as serious enough to send one of its own case workers to visit the family. He emphasizes that the department agrees with the school that Jody needs improved home supervision given his difficulties in class. Convincing Mrs. Williams of the school's legitimate concern, she agrees to meet with the school's social worker and nurse to discuss the proposed plan designed to help Jody and the family.

Appendix G:
SOURCES OF INFORMATION

American Humane Association
Children's Division
P. O. Box 1266
Denver, Colorado 80201

Child Care Information Center
532 Settlers Landing Road
P. O. Box 548
Hampton, Virginia 23669

Child Welfare League of America, Inc.
67 Irving Place
New York, New York 10003

National Center for the Prevention and Treatment
    of Child Abuse and Neglect
University of Colorado Medical Center
1205 Onedia Street
Denver, Colorado 80220

National Center for Voluntary Action
1785 Massachusetts Avenue, N.W.
Washington, D.C. 20036

National Center on Child Abuse and Neglect
United States Children's Bureau
Office of Child Development, DHEW
Washington, D.C. 20013

Region I: Connecticut, Maine, Massachusetts,
New Hampshire, Rhode Island, Vermont

New England Resource Center for
Children and Families
Judge Baker Guidance Center
295 Longwood Avenue
Boston, MA 02115

Region II: Resource Center on
Children and Youth

Cornell University
Family Life Development Center
College of Human Ecology
Ithaca, NY 14853

Region III: Delaware, Maryland, Pennsylvania,
Virginia, West Virginia, District of Columbia

Associate Regional Commissioner, CS
Gateway Building, DHEW/SRS, 36th & Market
Post Office Box 7760
Philadelphia, Pennsylvania 19101

Region IV: Alabama, Florida, Georgia,
Kentucky, Mississippi, North Carolina,
South Carolina, Tennessee

Southeastern Regional Resource Center
for Children and Youth Services
University of Tennessee
School of Social Work
1838 Terrace Avenue
Knoxville, TN 37996-3920

Region V : Illinois, Indiana, Michigan, Minnesota,
Ohio, Wisconsin

Region V Resource Center on Children
and Youth Services
School of Social Welfare
University of Wisconsin-Milwaukee
P.O. Box 786
Milwaukee, WI 53201

Region VI: Arkansas, Louisiana, New Mexico,
Oklahoma, Texas

Region VI Resource Center for Children,
Youth and Families
University of Texas at Austin
Austin, TX 78712

Region VII: Iowa, Kansas, Missouri, Nebraska

Region VII Children, Youth and Family
Resources Center Institute of Child
Behavior and Development
University of Iowa
Oakdale, Iowa 32319

Region VIII: Colorado, Montana, North
Dakota, South Dakota, Utah, Wyoming

Region VIII Family Resource Center
Graduate School of Social Work
University of Denver
Denver, Colorado 80208

Region IX: Arizona, California, Hawaii,
Nevada, Guam, Trust Territory of Pacific
Islands, American Somoa

Region IX Consolidated Resource Center
for Children and Youth Services
California State University
5151 State University Drive
Los Angeles, CA 90032

Region X: Alaska, Idaho, Oregon, Washington

Northwest Resource Center for
Children, Youth and Families
University of Washington
School of Social Work
4101 - 15th Avenue N.E.
Seattle, WA 98195

National Coalition for Children's Justice
66 Witherspoon Street
Princeton, NJ 08540

National Committee for Prevention of Child Abuse
Suite 510
111 East Wacker Drive
Chicago, Illinois 60601

Parental Stress Service, Inc.
154 Santa Clara Avenue
Oakland, California 94610

Parents Anonymous
National Office
2810 Artesia Boulevard
Redondo Beach, California 90278

Appendix H:
AN ANNOTATED LISTING
OF FILMS AND FILMSTRIPS

The Battered Child (physical abuse and neglect)
bw/58 min./Catalog No. CS1977
Produced by National Educational Television, 1969
This is a documentary study of child abuse based on the
book *The Battered Child* by Drs. C. Henry Kempe and Ray
E. Helfer. Contact: Indiana University, Audio-Visual Center, Bloomington, IN 47401 (812) 337-8087.

Abused Adolescents Speak Out (sexual abuse)
bw/1/2" videotape/26 min.
Produced by Face to Face Health and Counseling Service,
Inc., St. Paul, Minn.
In this videotaped group discussion among 4 abused adolescents and a counselor, the 4 recount their experiences
and emphasize the importance of having someone to talk
to and someplace to go to get away from the abusive home
situation. They all had feelings of helplessness and of somehow deserving the maltreatment. The unedited, graphic
language and descriptions of the victims' experiences make
this program suitable for training professionals who deal
with adolescents. Contact: Face to Face Health and Counseling Service, Inc., 730 Mendota, St. Paul, MN 55106

*A Time for Caring: The School's Response to the Sexually
Abused Child.*
Produced by Profile Films, 1978
color 16mm film/28 min/or 3/4" videocassette
Various procedures and models are presented in the recognition, reporting, and follow through of sexual abuse in
children for school personnel. Through a series of interviews with a social worker, principal, nurse, physician, and
counselor, background and a definition of sexual abuse are
provided along with physical and behavioral indicators.
Also included are testimonies of women sexually abused as
children, who share their feelings and provide insights into
the stigma of sexual abuse. Contact: Lawren productions,
Inc., P.O. Box 666, Mendocino, CA 95460.

Child Abuse: Police Intervention (law)
26 min./Catalog No. DM11
Produced by Cavalcade Productions, 1980
The police role in a child abuse case often means a difficult and sensitive intervention. This film presents three
situations which dramatize the problems confronting law
enforcement officers. The film illustrates the multi-disci-
plinary cooperation needed among the police, protective
services, school personnel, and medical professionals. The
film is accompanied by a Leader's Guide, authored by Dr.
Barry Schreiber, noted authority on crisis intervention and
professor at the Center for Studies in Criminal Justice, St.
Cloud State University. Contact: MTI Teleprograms Inc.,
3710 Commercial Ave., Northbrook, IL 60062 (800) 323-
5343.

Child Abuse: Cradle of Violence (treatment)
color / 20 min.
Produced by Mitchel-Gebhardt Film Co. for Bonanza Films, 1976
The film takes a differnt look at child abuse and its prevention. Parents discuss direction provided by self-help groups of former abusive parents and by community services such as parental stress hot lines and classes teaching parental skills. In Arkansas, Kansas, Louisiana, Missouri, Oklahoma, and Texas, contact: Motorola Teleprograms, Inc. / 7919 Cliffbrook Drive / Suite 243 / Dallas, TX 75240, or call collect (214) 661-8464. In Alaska, Hawaii, and Illinois, contact: Motorola Teleprograms, Inc. / 4825 N. Scott Screet / Suite 23 / Schiller Park, IL 60176, or call collect (312) 671-0141. In all other states, contact: the Illinois address, or call toll-free (800) 323-1900.

Child Molesters: Fact and Fiction (sexual abuse)
color / 30 min.
Produced in 1976 by Summerhill Productions, Toronto
Documenting information about molesters, the film analyzes pedophilia, showing examples from typical cases. A group discusses myths contrasted to facts about child molesters. Contact: AIMS Media, Inc., 626 Justin Ave., Glendale, CA 91201.

Children in Peril (physical abuse and neglect)
color / 22 min.
Produced by ABC-TV, 1975.
This film reports that, according to medical authorities,

the leading cause of infant death in the United States may well be murder at the hands of the infant's own parents. According to the film, there were some 60,000 reported cases of child abuse in the United States in 1974, and an estimated two children die of abuse each day in this country alone. The film also reveals that child abusers are not strikingly different from nonabusive adults. Contact: Xerox Films / Xerox Educational Publications / 245 Long Hill Road / Middletown, CT 06457 / (203) 347-7251.

Cipher in the Snow (emotional abuse)
color / 24 min.
Produced by Brigham Young University, 1973
An award-winning film, this dramatization of psychological abuse is based on the true story of a boy no one thought was important until his sudden death one snowy morning. Contact: Brigham Young University / Media Marketing W-STAD / Provo, UT 84602 / (801) 374-1211, Ext. 4071.

Daddy Doesn't Live Here Anymore: The Single-Parent Family (divorce)
color / four-part filmstrip-tape program / Catalog No. 741-00-CSG
This program examines factors that are making single-parent families so commonplace, and explores the dynamics of living in non-traditional families. Using dramatizations based on actual case histories, the program depicts the problems and satisfactions of learning to manage a family without the presence of a spouse. Part 1—The

Changing Family documents the startling demographic changes that have taken place in the status of the American family. Part 2—When Parents Divorce explores the personal consequences of divorce. Part 3—One Day at a Time presents the day-to-day realities of running a single-parent household. Part 4—The Stepparent Family examines the special complications that may result when a parent's remarriage creates a stepparent family. Contact: Human Relations Media, 175 Tompkins Ave., Pleasantville, NY 10570 (800) 431-2050.

Don't Give Up On Me (social workers)
color / 28 min.
Produced by Cavalcade Productions, 1975.
Accompanied by an instructor's manual and useful for social workers, the film's emphasis is on understanding and helping parents so overwhelmed by problems that they lash out at their youngsters. Only one character in the case, a social worker, is played by a professional actor. Therapists, counselors, and abusive parents and their children play themselves. In Arkansas, Kansas, Louisiana, Missouri, Oklahoma, and Texas, contact: Motorola Teleprograms, Inc. / 7919 Cliffbrook Drive / Suite 243 / Dallas, TX 75240, or call collect (214) 661-8464. In Alaska, Hawaii, and Illinois, contact: Motorola Teleprograms, Inc. / 4825 North Scott Street / Suite 23 / Schiller Park, IL 60176, or call collect (312) 671-0141. In all other states, contact: the Illinois address or call toll-free (800) 323-1900.

Double Jeopardy (sexual abuse)
Produced by Cavalcade Productions, Inc., Wheaton, IL
1978.
color 16mm film or 3/4" videocassette / 40 min.
Several cases of sexual assault are followed to illustrate
the numerous interviews, disbelief, prolonged adjudica-
tion, and demeaning cross-examination to which child
victims are subjected. The need for professionals to
understand the child's embarrassment, the dynamics of
sexual abuse, and child developmental stages is stressed.
Preparation for and techniques of interviewing are reviewed, as well as a prosecutor's case preparation and
courtroom techniques. The importance and role of the
child advocate are also discussed. Contact: MTI Teleprograms, Inc., 3710 Commercial Ave., Northbrook, IL
60062

Fragile—Handle with Care (overview of child abuse and
neglect)
color / 26 min. / Free Loan
Produced by KTAR-TV Productions in cooperation with
the Independent Order of the Foresters, 1975.
Narrated by Bill Cosby, the film shows that abuse of children is an old but increasing problem and examines why
parents abuse their children and what happens to the children, both physically and mentally. The film looks at ways
of preventing child abuse and deals with the legal consider-

ations involved. The situations portrayed are reenactments of authentic case histories. Contact: Mr. James Martin / High Court of Southern California / 100 Border Avenue / Solana Beach, CA 92075 (714) 755-5158.

Incest: The Hidden Crime (sexual abuse)
color / 16 min.
Produced by: CBS News, 1979.
A documentary film which examines the nature and extent of incest in this nation. Incest is described as one of society's best kept secrets. The film encourages informed awareness among viewers: its message being that the secrecy surrounding incest must be brought into the open and dealt with. Contact: The Media Guild / 11526 Sorrento Valley Rd. / Suite J / San Diego, CA 92121.

Incest: The Victim Nobody Believes (sexual abuse)
color / 23 min.
Produced by Mitchel-Gebhardt Film Co., 1976.
This documentary film creates an awareness of the problem of sexual assault on children. Three victims of incest tell their stories of fear, confusion, isolation, and guilt. Contact: J. Gary Mitchell Film Co. / 2000 Bridgeway / Sausalito, CA 94965 / (415) 332-5760.

Incest: Tom Snyder's Tomorrow Show (sexual abuse)
color 3/4" videocassette / 50 min
Produced by NBC TV, Los Angeles, CA, 1977.
Dr. Frank Ossanka and an incest victim, Sheila, are interviewed. A technical discussion and definition of sexual

abuse are presented, and Sheila discusses her own sexual abuse within her foster home and the guilt feelings she experienced. Dr. Henry Giaretto, Dorothy (a staff member of the Child Sexual Abuse Treatment Program, San Jose, California), and an incest offender are also interviewed. They discuss the role and therapy program of the CSATP. Some statistics and general patterns in sexual abuse cases are indicated. The incest offender tells about his incestual relationship with his daughter, his treatment, and recovery. Contact: Regional .Institute of Social Welfare Research, Inc. / P.O. Box 152 Heritage Bldg. / 468 N. Milledge Ave., Athens, GA 30601

Is That What You Want for Yourself? (teen sexuality)
color / 13 min. / LC #80-701294
Produced by Health Video Services, 1980
Fifteen-year-old Debbie Edwards, one of four children of a Brooklyn, New York family, is trying to deal with her sexuality and the problems presented by the possibility of teenage pregnancy: whether to be sexually active, to have a baby, to get married, to quit school, and whether or not to be honest with the other members of her family. The film is designed to trigger discussion as it honestly presents the dilemmas. Purposely left open-ended, the film makes no judgments and condemns no one. Contact: Learning Corporation of America, 1350 Avenue of the Americas, New York, NY 10102.

The Last Taboo (sexual abuse)
color / 30 min.
Produced by Cavalcade Productions, 1977.
Intended for public information, this film explains sexual

abuse of children, including the effects on and the feelings of the victim. In Arkansas, Kansas, Louisiana, Missouri, Oklahoma, and Texas, contact: Motorola Teleprograms, Inc. / 7919 Cliffbrook Drive / Suite 243 / Dallas, TX 75240, or call collect (214) 661-8464. In Alaska, Hawaii, and Illinois, contact: Motorola Teleprograms, Inc. / 4825 North Scott Street / Suite 23 / Schiller Park, IL 60176, or call collect (312) 671-0141. In all other states, contact: the Illinois address, or call toll-free (800) 323-1900.

Lift a Finger: The Teacher's Role in Combating Child Abuse and Neglect
This is a three part presentation of the child abuse and neglect problem which consists of four (4) slide trays and three (3) accompanying tapes. Prepared for use by school personnel in the state of Texas, it nevertheless offers a useful analysis of the problem and a suggested range of strategies helpful to professionals in other states. The program covers three topics: (1) An overview of child abuse; (2) Identification and referral, and (3) Legal aspects. A detailed study guide, including evaluation instruments, accompanies the program. Persons offering in-service workshops for teachers and school staff will find it a helpful resource. Contact: Consortium C / 1750 Seamist Box 863 / Houston, TX 77008

Little Bear (sexual abuse)
45 in. / date unknown
Produced by Bridgework Theater Inc., Goshen, IN
This play, which is part of The Bridgework Theater's Education for the Prevention of Sexual Abuse project, is designed for elementary school children. The program uses animal characters to educate children about sexual and physical abuse and their prevention.

My Parents Are Getting a Divorce
Two-part filmstrip-tape program / Catalog No. 618-00-CSG / 1976
This program examines divorce in today's society and some of the reasons behind the high divorce rate. It discusses the problems teenagers and other family members may encounter when divorce seems imminent. Part 1 — Separation explains that the causes of divorce are often very complex and cannot be attributed to one parent. Part 2 — Adjusting discusses how teens can cope with feelings of rejection and encourages them to help younger children and parents build happier lives. Contact: Human Relations Media, 175 Tompkins Ave., Pleasantville, NY 10570 (800) 431-2050.

Mommy, Daddy and Us Kids (parenting)
color / 50 min., or 31 min.
Produced by Ralph Graham, M.D., 1974.
Available in either a long or short version, this film shows successful techniques in treating family problems and examines both the responsibilities of parents and the effects

of environment on the development of children. Contact: Cine VIP Co. / P.O. Box 2278 / Orange, CA 92669 / (714) 639-6321.

No Easy Answers (sexual abuse)
60 min. play / date unknown
Produced by Illusion Theater, Minneapolis, MN
In this play, young people are offered prevention information on sexual abuse. The program is suggested for junior and senior high school students. Contact: Nancy Riestenberg, Illusion Theater, 528 Hennepin Ave. #309, Minneapolis, MN 55403

Ordinary People
25 min. / Catalog # UP01
Produced by Artemis Productions, 1977
Shows how normal stresses can combine to place an average normal parent in danger of behaving abusively toward his or her children. Focuses on a family in which the mother's feelings of isolation contributes to her inability to cope with her 9-year-old son and infant daughter. Points out the distress signals of child abuse: the persistent, unexplained crying of the baby, the mother's unrealistically high expectations for her children, mysterious bruises on the son, and the mother's ambivalence and recurring avoidance in her contacts with the public health nurse. Contact: MTI Teleprograms, Inc., 3710 Commercial Avenue, Northbrook, IL 60062 (800) 323-5343.

Parenting: Growing with Children (parenting)
color / 22 min.
Produced by Peter Schnitzler, 1976.
Through four families, the film looks at the realities, rewards, and responsibilities of being parents. Contact: Film Fair Communications, 10900 Ventura Boulevard / Studio City, CA 91604 (213) 985-0244.

Raised in Anger
color / 54 min.
Produced by WQED-TV, 1979
This film discusses child abuse, and treatment and prevention programs. Explodes several of the myths generally associated with child abuse. Describes fantasies and misconceptions about raising children, highlighting the increasing frustration, isolation and general stresses of modern living that can lead to child abuse. With Edward Asner as Host and Commentator. Contact: The Media Guild, 118 S. Acacia, Box 881, Solana Beach, CA 92075.

Reward and Punishment (parenting)
color / 14 min.
Produced by Peter Jordan, 1974.
The principles of reward and punishment are outlined by Dr. James Gardner, child psychologist. He discusses the use and abuse of punishment, its positive applications as well as negative effects. Contact: CRM McGraw-Hill Films, Del Mar, CA 92014 (714) 481-8184.

Running Away to What? (runaway children)
color 16mm film / 16 min. / or color videotape / 16 min.
Producted by National Broadcasting Co., Inc., New York,
NY, 1979
Teenagers who have run away from home to Fort Lauderdale, Florida, considered a mecca for teenage runaways,
are shown. The likelihood that teenage runaways will turn
to a life of crime is emphasized, and instances of several
runaways involved in crime and prostitution for survival
are depicted. It is noted that many of the teenagers run
away because life at home is intolerable. Runaways occu-
pying an empty motel in Ft. Lauderdale advise teenagers
considering running away to stay at home if possible.
Contact: Films Inc., 1144 Wilmette Ave., Wilmette, IL
60091.

*The Sexually Abused Child: A Protocol for Criminal
Justice*
color 16mm film / 26 min. / or 3/4" videocassette
Produced by Profile Films, 1979
Designed for law enforcement personnel, this film offers
suggestions for the prosecution of offenders while dealing
considerately with the victims of child rape, molestation,
and incest. The legal aspects of reporting and procedures
for reporting are included. Comments from law enforcement officers, social workers, educators, attorneys, physicians, judges, and probation, corrections and receiving
home personnel illustrate the complex considerations in

dealing with the trauma of sexual abuse. Coordination of these professionals is shown to be effective in working with the victims, families, and offenders. Contact: Lawren Productions, Inc., P.O. Box 666, Mendocino, CA 95460.

The Sexually Abused Child: Identification/Interview
color / 10 min. / Catalog No. DH09
Produced by Cavalcade Productions, 1978
This film is a training aid for school and guidance personnel. It demonstrates various interviewing techniques when sexual abuse is suspected. A spontaneous, unrehearsed interview illustrates the interaction between a child and the professional. The film examines methods of establishing rapport, interpreting nonverbal cues, and dealing with the child's protective feelings toward the abuser. Instructor's Manual. Contact: MTI Teleprograms, Inc., 3710 Commercial Ave., Northbrook, IL 60062 / (800) 323-5343.

Sexual Abuse of Children: America's Secret Shame
color / 28 min. / sd / Catalog No. CSC-2908
Produced by TGL Productions, AIMS, 1980.
Provides an in-depth look at the surprising extent of sexual child abuse in America and examines what can be done about the problem. FEatures interviews with experts (educators, law enforcement people, and district attorneys), past victims who are now teenagers, and convicted child molesters. Gives explanations of who the child molesters are, how they lure innocent children, and how

victims usually suffer emotional damage the rest of their lives. Narrated by Peter Graves. Contact: AIMS Media, Inc., 626 Justin Ave., Glendale, CA 91201

Teenage Mother: A Broken Dream
color / 14 min. / Catalog No. 10054 / 1977
Provocative portrait of an unwed 15-year-old mother in Grand Rapids, Michigan. She explains why she wanted a baby and expresses her hopes for the future—though in a mordant postscript we learn that she is in a detention home and her baby is in an orphanage. Includes interviews with her mother and with the director of a progressive school for pregnant high school students. Contact: University of California / Extension Media Center / 2223 Fulton St. / Berkeley, CA 94720 / (415) 642-0460.

Teenage Parents
color / 10 min. / Code 16mm 106818X
Produced by CBS News, 1981.
This film documents the lifestyles of two teenaged married couples who are discovering what it is like to assume the responsibilities of marriage and parenthood while still teenagers. Produced by CBS News. Contact: CRM / McGraw-Hill Films, 110 Fifteenth St., Del Mar, CA 92014.

Teenage Pregnancy and Prevention
three part filmstrip-tape / also available in sound / slide with carousel trays / Catalog No. 632-00-CSG / 1980.
Examining why teenage pregnancy has reached epidemic

proportions, this three-part program discusses the emotional, social and economic difficulties that face teenage parents. Students examine the reasons behind this growing problem and learn that mature sexual attitudes and greater sexual responsibility are necessary to its control. Part 1 — The Problem uses statistics to dramatically underscore the magnitude of a problem which has drastically increased in recent years. Part 2 — The Choices illustrates, through sensitive case studies, the range of difficult choices that pregnant teenagers must make, among them having the baby alone, marriage, abortion, adoption, foster care. Part 3 — The Solutions emphasizes that accurate information about sex and birth control is the most powerful means of reducing teenage pregnancies and also provides a foundation for more mature attitudes about sontact: Human Relations Media / 175 Tompkins Ave. / Pleasantville, NY 10570 / (800) 431-2050.

This Child is Rated X (law)
color / 52 min.
Produced by NBC-TV, 1972
This is a study of the abused child's rights and the inequities of juvenile justice in four states. Contact: Films, Inc. / 1144 Wilmette Avenue / Wilmette, IL 60091 (312) 256-6600.

Touch (sexual abuse)
60 min. play / date unknown
Produced by Illusion Theater, Minneapolis, MN
This sexual abuse education program gives children the opportunity to consider various types of touch: touch that

is nurturing, delightful, and-or funny; and touch that is confusing, uncomfortable, and-or exploitive. The program is suggested for students in kindergarten through eighth grade. Contact: Illusion Theater / 528 Hennepin Ave. #309 / Minneapolis, MN 55403.

Violence in the Family
four-part filmstrip-tape / also available in sound/slide with carousel trays / Catalog No. 636-00-CSG / 1978.
This comprehensive and sensitive program examines the causes, characteristics and possible solutions to family violence—a major social problem which we are just beginning to understand. Part 1—Dynamics of Family Violence presents the many reasons for the widespread violence in American Families. Part 2—Child Abuse and Neglect explores the prevalence of harm done to children, and probes the motivations of abusive, neglectful parents and their effects on the growing child. Part 3—Battered Wives studies the causes of wife beating and the historical roots of violence against women. Part 4—Adolescence Abuse charts the widespread incidence of adolescent abuse and its effects on teenage victims. Contact: Human Relations Media / 175 Tompkins Ave. / Pleasantville, NY 10570 / (800) 431-2050.

War of Eggs (causes, physical abuse and neglect)
color and bw / 27 min.
Produced by Paulist Productions, 1971.
Written by Michael Crichton and starring Elizabeth Ashley and Bill Bixby, this film is a sensitive dramatization of the

child battering syndrome, focusing on the husband-wife relationship. Contact: Paulist Productions / P.O. Box 1057 / Pacific Palisades, CA 90272 / (213) 454-0688.

Who Do You Tell?
color / 11 min. / Catalog No. GM09
Produced by J.G. Mitchell; MTI, 1978.
Uses animation and live action to discuss the support systems available to children when they are confronted with problems of safety, abuse, or molestation. Points out that the people causing the problem may be relatives or friends rather than strangers. Deals with personal feelings of guilt or fear which may present conflicts in finding help. Contact: MTI Teleprograms, Inc. / 3710 Commercial Ave. / Northbrook, IL 60062 / (800) 323-5343.

Whose Child Is This?
color / 29 min. / LC #79-701414 / 1979
Increasing signs of withdrawal in one of the children in her class prompts a teacher to investigate the cause. Her discovery is that the child is a victim of physical abuse — beatings at the hands of her parents. Despite misgivings about becoming involved, the teacher's sense of responsibility leads her to take action, and the film takes the viewer on a dramatic journey through the legal steps which ensue. Produced by the Junior League of Louisville, Kentucky, the film presents one state's model for dealing with this problem. Contact: Learning Corporation of America / 1350 Avenue of the Americas, New York, NY 10102.

Woman: Sexual Abuse of Children
color 3/4" videocassette / 29 min.
Produced by WNED-TV / Buffalo, NY / 1977
Two social workers discuss the incidence of sexual abuse of children by family members and neighbors, and explain how to tell a child about molestation, how to identify the abuser, what parents can do to prevent it, how law enforcement officers respond to reports of sexual abuse, and effects of sexual abuse on children. The discussion includes family rehabilitation. Contact: PBS Video / 475 L'Enfant Plaza S.W., Washington, DC 20024.

Women of Valor: Family Aids to Battering Parents
Training Package
color / 31 min.
A dramatization, this film follows a child through the hospital, custody, and juvenile court system. With a manual and slides, the film shows how volunteer supervision of the home allows the child to return. Contact: Trikon Productions / P.O. Box 21 / LaJolla, CA 92038 / (714) 459-5233.

The Youngest Victim: America's Sexually
Exploited Child (sexual abuse)
color 3/4" videocassette / 60 min
Produced by KABC-TV, Los Angeles, CA / 1981
This documentary explores all aspects of child molestation, prostitution, and pornography. Two pedophiles discuss

their lives and their relationships with their child victims. Parents of children who have been molested describe the effect the experience has had on their lives. Victims are also interviewed. Law enforcement officials express their frustration about not being able to keep molesters off the streets, even if they do receive convictions due to current laws. The program also provides insight into how child molesters receive therapy at 2 California state hostpials. The need for stronger laws and more effective treatment for molesters as well as their victims is emphasized. Contact: Volt Productions / 4610 Van Nuys Blvd. / Sherman Oaks, CA 91403

Appendix I:
INEXPENSIVE OR FREE PAMPHLETS

Child Abuse and Neglect: Model Legislation for the States
   (Report No. 71)
Available from: Education Commission of the States
                  300 Lincoln Tower, 1860 Lincoln Street
                  Denver, Colorado 80203
   This pamphlet contains an examination of how legislation can improve state and local efforts to combat child
abuse and neglect. It encourages state legislators to review
their existing laws and revise them where appropriate.
Model legislation is suggested and is accompanied by a text
explaining why certain provisions are included.

*Education Policies and Practices Regarding Child Abuse
   and Neglect, and Recommendations for Policy Development* (Report No. 85)
Available from: Education Commission of the States
   This phamphlet reports on the findings of a survey
aimed at assessing the frequency of policy development at
state and local levels in the area of child abuse and neglect.
A suggested policy statement with detailed explanation of
each of its components is included.

Education for Parenthood: A Primary Prevention Strategy for Child Abuse and Neglect (Report No. 93)
Available from: Education Commission of the States

This pamphlet examines parenting education as a potentially useful strategy in combating child abuse and neglect. A rationale for parent education is included along with a suggested plan of action aimed at initiating curriculum development in this area of study.

Guidelines for Schools: Teachers, Nurses, Counselors and Administrators
Available from: The Children's Division of
               the American Humane Association
               P.O. Box 1266
               Denver, Colorado 80201

This pamphlet provides a brief but useful review of the child abuse and neglect problem with an emphsis on how school personnel can assist in the resolution of the problem. A list of "indicators" is identified dealing with both the child's behavior and appearance as well as typical parental attitudes which might suggest abusive or negligent treatment.

A Look at Child Abuse
Available from: National Committee for Prevention of
               Child Abuse
               Suite 510
               111 East Wacker Drive
               Chicago, Illinois 60601

This pamphlet is written in laymen's language and is helpful for teachers, volunteers, physicians, troubled parents and students who want to become acquainted with the problem. Its chapters include: "What is Abuse," "Chilhood's Seamy Past," "Looking for Causes," "Child Abuse and the Law," "Ways to Stop Child Abuse," and "Blueprint for Action."

Appendix J:
REFERENCES AND BIBLIOGRAPHY

Ackerman, F.J. *Children of Alcoholics.* Second Edition. Holmes Beach, Florida: Learning Publications, Inc., 1984.

Alan Guttmacher Institute, *Teenage Pregnancy: The Problem That Hasn't Gone Away.* Alan Guttmacher Institute, 360 Park Avenue South, NY, NY 10010, 1981.

Anastasiow, Nicholas J., et. al. *The Adolescent Parent,* Baltimore: Paul H. Brookes Publishing Co., 1982.

Bakan, D. *Slaughter of the Innocents.* San Francisco: Jossey-Bass, 1971.

Berg, B. et. al. "In Health-Related Tasks, Where Does the School Nurse Function?" *Journal of SChool Health,* May, 1973.

Bolton, Frank G. Jr., *The Pregnant Adolescent: Problems of Premature Parenthood.* Beverly Hills: Sage Publications, 1980.

Bourne, Richard and Newberg, Eli H. (Editors), *Critical Perspectives on Child Abuse.* Lexington, MA: Lexington Books, 1980.

Broadhurst, D. "Project Protection: A School Program to Detect and Prevent Child Abuse and Neglect." *Children Today,* Vol. 4, 1975.

Brody, H. and Gaiss, B. "Ethical Issues in Screening for Unusual Child-Rearing Practices." *Pediatric Annals,* Vol. 5, No. 3, March, 1976.

Bronfenbrenner, U. (Ed.), *Influences on Human Development.* New York: Holt, Rinehard and Winston, Inc., 1972.

Brookover, W. and Erickson, E. L. *Sociology of Education,* Homewood, Illinois: Dorsey Press, 1975.

Campbell, Arthur A., "Trends in Teenage Childbearing in the United States." Found in Catherine S. Chilman, editor, *Adolescent Pregnancy and Childbearing: Findings from Research.* U.S. Department of Health and Human Services, Public Health Service, National Institutes of Health, December 1980.

Caskey, O.L. and Richardson, I. "Understanding and Helping Child-Abusing Parents." *Elementary School Guidance and Counseling,* March, 1975.

Chase, N.F. *A Child is Being Beaten: Violence Against Children; An American Tragedy.* Holt, 1975.

"Child Sexual Abuse: Incest, Assault, and Sexual Exploitation," DHHS Publication No. 81-30166, Revised, 1981.

Children Today, May-June, 1975.

Clements, T.J. "Child Abuse: The Problem of Definition." *Creighton Law Review,* Vol. 8, No. 4, June, 1975.

Cohen, S. J. *A National Survey of Attitudes of Selected Professionals Involved in the Reporting of Child Abuse and Neglect.* New York: Juvenile Standards Project, Institute of Judicial Administration, Inc., 1974.

Daniel, J.H. et al. "Child Abuse Screening: Implications of the Limited Predictive Power of Abuse Discriminants From a Controlled Family Study of Pediatric Social Illness." Society of Research in Child Development Biannual Meeting, New Orleans, LA, March, 1977.

Darabi, Katherine F., "A Closer Look at Schooling After the First Birth." *Journal of School Health,* March 1982, Vol. 52, No. 3 (pp 168-172).

DeFrancis, V. *The Fundamentals of Child Protection: A Statement of Basic Concepts and Principles.* Denver: The American Humane Association, Children's Division, 1955.

Demanse, L. "Our Forebears Made Childhood a Nightmare." *Psychology Today,* April, 1975.

Drews, K. "The Child and His School." In R. Helfer and H. Kempe (Eds.), *Helping the Battered Child and His Family.* Philadelphia: J.B. Lippincott Co., 1972.

Ebeling, Nancy and Hill, Deborah, *Child Abuse and Neglect: A Guide with Case Studies for Treating the Child and Family.* Boston: John Wright • PSG Inc., 1983.

Ebeling, N. and Hill, D. *Child Abuse Intervention and Treatment,* Action, MA: Publishing Sciences Group, Inc., 1975.

Education Commission of the States. *Child Abuse and Neglect: Model Legislation for the States.* Denver, July, 1975.

Education Commission of the States. *Child Abuse and Neglect in the States: A Digest of Critical Elements of Reporting and Central Registries.* (Report No. 83), Denver, March, 1976.

Education Commission of the States. *Educational Policies and Practices Regarding Child Abuse.* (Report No. 85), Denver, 1976.

Education Commission of the States. *Teacher Education — An Active Participant in Solving the Problem of Child Abuse.* (Report No. 99), Denver, 1977.

Elmer, E. "Hazards in Determining Child Abuse." *Child Welfare,* Vol. 45, No. 1, 1966.

Elmer, E. and Gregg, G. "Developmental Characteristics of Abused Children." *Pediatrics,* Vol. 40, 1967.

Faller, Kathleen C., *Social Work with Abused and Neglected Children: A Manual of Interdisciplinary practice.* New York: Free Press, 1981.

Ferro, F. "Protecting Children: The National Center on Child Abuse and Neglect." *Childhood Education,* November-December, 1975.

Finklehor, David, *Sexually Victimized Children.* New York: Free Press, 1979.

Fischer, Louis and David, Schimmel. *The Rights of Students and Teachers: Resolving Conflicts in the SChool Community.* New York: Harper and Row, Publishers, 1982.

Fischer, L. and Schimmel, D. *The Cigil Rights of Students.* New York: Harper and Row, 1975.

Fontana, V.J. "Factors Needed for Prevention of Child Abuse and Neglect." *Pediatrics,* Vol. 46, No. 2, 1970.

Fontana, V.J. "Which Parents Abuse Children?" *Medical Insight,* Vol. 3, No. 10, 1971.

Fontana, V.J. *Somewhere a Child Is Crying: Maltreatment Causes and Prevention.* New York: Macmillan, 1973.

Forrer, S. E. "Battered Children and Counselor Responsibility." *School Counselor,* Vol. 22, No. 3, January, 1975.

Garbarino, James, Stocking, Holly, and Associates, *Protecting Children From Abuse and Neglect.* Jossey-Bass, 1980.

Garbarino, James and Gillian, Gwen, *Understanding Abusive Families.* Lexington, MA: Lexington Books, 1980.

Gelles, Richard J., *Family Violence.* Beverly Hills, CA: Sage Publications, 1979.

Gil, D. G. "What Schools Can Do About Child Abuse." *American Education,* Vol. 5, April, 1969.

Gil, D. G. *Violence Against Children: Physical Child Abuse In the United States.* Cambridge, Mass: Harvard University Press, 1970.

Goldmeier, H. "School-age Parents and the Public Schools." *Children Today.* September-October, 1976.

Goodwin, Jean, *Sexual Abuse: Incest Victims and Their Families.* Boston: John Wright • PSG Inc., 1982.

Gottschalk, *Perspectives on Child Abuse: A Synthetic Approach to Public Policy Making.* Master's Thesis, California University at Berkeley, June, 1974.

Harmon, David and Brin Jr., Orville G., *Learning to be Parents: Principles, Programs and Methods.* Beverly Hills: Sage Publications, 1980.

Harriman, R. L., *Child Abuse and the School.* Doctoral Dissertation, University of the Pacific, Stockton, California, 1975.

Harrison, C. H. *Schoolgirl Pregnancy: Old Problem; New Solutions.* National School Public Relations Association Special Report, 1972.

Helfer, R.E. "Basic Issues Concerning Prediction." In: R. E. Helfer and C. H. Kempe (Eds.), *Child Abuse and Neglect: The Family and the Community.* Cambridge, Mass: Ballinger Publishing Co., 1976.

Helfer, R. E. and Kempe, C. H. (Eds.), *The Battered Child.* Chicago: The University of Chicago Press, 1st Ed. 1968, 2nd Ed. 1974.

Helfer, R. E. and Kempe, C. H. (Eds.), *Child Abuse and Neglect: The Family and the Community.* Cambridge, Mass: Ballinger Publishing Co., 1976.

Henderson, J. "Incest: A Synthesis of Data." *Canadian Psychiatric Association Journal,* Vol. 17, 1972.

Hill, D. ' Communication and Collaboration: Developing Approaches to Child Abuse, Prevention and Treatment." In: Fifth National Symposium on Child Abuse, Denver, Colorado: American Humane Association, 1976.

Holmes, S. Barnhart, C., Cantoni, L. and Reymer, E. "Working with the Parent in Child Abuse Cases." *Social Casework,* January, 1975.

Howard, M. "Pregnant School-age Girls." *Journal of School Health,* September, 1971.

Howard, M. "How Can Classroom Teachers Help?" *Today's Education,* February-March, 1978.

Jordan, C. E. "Educational Options in New Brunswick." *Today's Education,* February-March, 1978.

Kadushin, Alfred, and Martin, Judith, *Child Abuse: An Interactional Event.* New York: Columbia University Press, 1981.

Kamerman, S. B. and Harte, A. *Child Abuse and Neglect: Problems, Policies and Provision.* (Report No. 3) New York: Columbia University, School of Social Work, 1975.

Kaufman, I., Peck, A. and Tagiuri, C.K., "The Family Constellation and Overt Incestuous Relations Between Father and Daughter." *American Journal of Ortho-Psychiatry,* Vol. 24, 1954.

Kempe, C. H. "Arresting or Freezing the Developmental Process: Related Aspects in Child Psychiatry." In R. E. Helfer and C. H. Kempe (Eds.), *Child Abuse and Neglect: The Family and the Community.* Cambridge, Mass.: Ballinger Publishing Co., 1976.

Kempe, C. H. and Helfer, R. E. (Eds.), *Helping the Battered Child and His Family.* Philadelphia: J. B. Lippincott Co., 1972.

Kinsey, J. et al. *Sexual Behavior in the Human Female.* Philadelphia: Saunders Publishing, 1953.

Kline, D. F. and Christiansen, J. *Educational and Psychological Problems of Abused Children.* Washington, D.C.: USOE, DHEW Final Report, Contract No. G0075-00352, 1975.

Kline, D. F. *Child Abuse and Neglect: A Primer for School Personnel.* Reston, Virginia: The Council for Exceptional Children, 1977.

Leavitt, J. E. *The Battered Child: Selected Readings.* Morristown, N.J.: General Learning Press, 1974.

Light, R. "Abused and Neglected Children in America: A Study of Alternative Policies." *Harvard Educational Review,* Vol. 43, 1973.

Litwack, J. and Litwack, L. "The School Nurse as a Health Counselor." Journal of School Health, December, 1976.

Lynch, A. "Child Abuse in the School-age Population." *Journal of School Health,* Vol. 43, No. 3, March, 1975.

Maine Human Services Council. "Report and Recommendations on Child Abuse and Neglect." Augusta, Maine, 1976.

Martin, D. L. "The Growing Horror of Child Abuse and the Undeniable Role of the Schools in Putting an End to It." *American School Board Journal,* Vol. 160, November, 1973.

Martin, J. P. (Editor), *Violence and the Family.* New York: John Wiley and Sons, 1978.

Mayer, Adele, *The Sexual Abuse of Children,* Holmes Beach, FL: Learning Publications, Inc., 1984.

Mayer, Adele, *Incest.* Holmes Beach, FL: Learning Publications, Inc., 1983.

McAfee, O. and Nedler, S. *Education for Parenthood: A Primary Prevention Strategy for Child Abuse and Neglect.* (Report No. 93), Denver: Education Commission of the States, 1976.

McLaughlin, B. L. "Administrative Letter No. 65," State of Maine, Department of Education and Cultural Services, September 20, 1973.

McQuiston, M. "Crisis Nurseries." In H. Q. Martin (Ed.), *The Abused Child: A Multidisciplinary Approach to Developmental Issues and Treatment.* Cambridge, Mass.: Ballinger Publishing Co., 1976.

Meier, J. H. "Symposium on Prevention: Helping Parents Parent." In *Proceedings of the First National Conference on Child Abuse and Neglect.* Athens, Georgia: Regional Institute of Social Welfare Research, 1977.

Mondale, W. F. "The Burdened Family." *Trial Magazine,* May-June, 1974.

Mott, Frank L., and Maxwell, Nora L., "School-age Mothers: 1968-1979." *Family Planning Perspectives.* Vol. 13, No. 6, Nov.-Dec. 1981.

Murdoc, C. G. "The Abused Child and the School System." *American Journal of Public Health,* Vol. 60, No. 1, 1970.

Nagi, S. *Child Maltreatment in the United States.* New York: Columbia University Press, 1977.

National Center on Child Abuse and Neglect. *Multidisciplinary Teams in Child Abuse and Neglect Programs.* U.S. DHEW, Publication No. OHDS 78-30152, 1978.

National Federation of Settlements and Neighborhood Centers. *Education for Parenthood Programs.* Final Report: DHEW, 1976.

Parker, N. "The School Nurse." *Today's Education,* Vol. 63, No. 4, November-December, 1974.

Paulsen, M. G. "Legal Protection Against Child Abuse." *Children,* Vol. 13, 1966.

Pelton, Leroy, *The Social Context of Child Abuse and Neglect.* New York: Human Services Press, 1981.

Peters, H. J. "Counseling Children in the Elementary School." In D. C. Dinkmeyer (Ed.), *Guidance and Counseling in the Elementary School: Readings in Theory and Practice.* New York: Holt, Rinehart and Winston, Inc., 1968.

Pfohl, S. J. "The Discovery of Child Abuse." *Social Problems,* Vol. 24, No. 3, 1977.

Phipps-Yonas, Susan, "Teenage Pregnancy and Motherhood: A Review of the Literature." *American Journal of Orthopsychiatry.* 50 (3), July, 1980.

Plummer, Carol A., *Preventing Sexual Abuse: Activities and Strategies for Those Working with Children and Adolescents.* Holmes Beach, FL: Learning Publications, Inc., 1984.

Polansky, N. A. *Child Neglect: Understanding and Reaching Parents.* New York: Dodd, Mead and Co., 1974.

Polansky, N. A., Hally, C., and Poilansky, N. F. *Profile of Neglect: A Survey of the State of Knowledge of Child Neglect.* U.S. DHEW, 1975.

Robinson, Bryan, and Barret, Robert L., "Issues and Problems Related to the Research on Teenage Fathers: A Critical Analysis." *The Journal of School Health.* Vol. 52, No. 10, December 1982.

Schmitt, B. D. "What Teachers Need to Know About Child Abuse and Neglect." *Childhood Education,* November-December, 1975.

Schultz, Leroy, *The Sexual Victimology of Youth.* Springfield, IL: Charles C. Thomas, 1980.

Sgroi, S. "Sexual Molestation of Children." *Children Today,* Vol. 4, 1975.

Shanas, B. "Child Abuse: A Killer Teachers Can Help Control." *Phi Delta Kappan,* March, 1975.

Silver, L. B., Barton, W. and Dublin, C. C. "Child Abuse Laws - Are They Enough? *Journal of the American Medical Association,* Vol. 199, No. 2, 1967.

Smith, Peggy B., Weinman, Maxine L., Mumford, David M., "Social and Affective Factors Associated with Adolescent Pregnancy." *The Journal of School Health,* February 1982, Vol. 52, No. 2 (pp 90-93).

Smith, R. C. "New Ways to Help Battering Parents." *Today's Health,* January, 1973.

Soeffing, M. "Abused Children are Exceptional Children." *Exceptional Children,* November, 1975.

Steele, B. F. and Polloc, C. B. "A Psychiatric Study of Parents Who Abuse Infants and Small Children." In R. Helfer and C. H. Kempe (Eds.), *The Battered Child.* Chicago: University of Chicago Press, 1968.

Straus, Murray A., Gelles, Richard J., Steinmetz, Suzanne K., *Behind Closed Doors: Violence in the Family.* Garden City, NY: Anchor Press/Doubleday, 1980.

Talen, T., DeFrank, C. and Gamm, S. *Child Abuse and Neglect Legal Handbook.* Chicago: Child Advocate Association, 1978.

Thorman, George, *Incestuous Families.* Springfield, IL: Charles C. Thomas, 1983.

U.S. Department of Health, Education and Welfare. *Child Abuse and Neglect: The Problem and Its Management.* Vols. 1-3, DHEW. Publication Nos. 75-30073-74-30075, 1975.

U.S. Department of Health, Education and Welfare. Interdisciplinary Glossary on Child Abuse and Neglect: Legal, Medical, Social Work Terms. *DHEW Publication No. 78-30137, 1978.*

Wald, M., "The Role of Schools in Child Protective Services," *Guidelines for Pupil Services,* Vol. 10, No. 3, May, 1972.

Wasserman, S. "The Abused Parent of the Abused Child." *Children,* Vol. 14, 1967.

Young, L. *Wednesday's Children: A Study of Child Neglect and Abuse.* New York: McGraw-Hill, 1964.

Zellman, Gail L., "Public School Programs for Adolescent Pregnancy and Parenthood: An Assessment." *Family Planning Perspectives.* Vol. 14, No. 1, Jan-Feb. 1982.

Index